DATE DUE

COUNTRIES OF THE WORLD

Afghanistan

Gareth Stevens Publishing
A WORLD ALMANAC EDUCATION GROUP COMPANY

About the Author: Halima Kazem was born in Kabul, Afghanistan, and raised in San Jose, California. She has a master's degree in Business and Economic Journalism from New York University. Kazem is currently working as a financial journalist in New York City.

Written by
HALIMA KAZEM

Edited by
KATHARINE BROWN

Edited in the U.S. by
**CATHERINE GARDNER
ALAN WACHTEL**

Designed by
ROSIE FRANCIS

Picture research by
SUSAN JANE MANUEL

First published in North America in 2003 by
Gareth Stevens Publishing
A World Almanac Education Group Company
330 West Olive Street, Suite 100
Milwaukee, Wisconsin 53212 USA

Please visit our web site at:
www.garethstevens.com
For a free color catalog describing
Gareth Stevens Publishing's list of high-quality
books and multimedia programs, call
1-800-542-2595 (USA) or 1-800-387-3178 (Canada).
Gareth Stevens Publishing's fax: (414) 332-3567.

© **TIMES MEDIA PRIVATE LIMITED 2003**
Originated and designed by
Times Editions
An imprint of Times Media Private Limited
A member of the Times Publishing Group
Times Centre, 1 New Industrial Road
Singapore 536196
http://www.timesone.com.sg/te

Library of Congress Cataloging-in-Publication Data
Kazem, Halima.
Afghanistan / by Halima Kazem.
p. cm. — (Countries of the world)
Summary: Discusses the geography, history, government, economy, people, politics, and culture of Afghanistan.
Includes bibliographical references and index.
ISBN 0-8368-2357-5 (lib. bdg.)
1. Afghanistan—Juvenile literature. [1. Afghanistan.] I. Title.
II. Countries of the world. (Milwaukee, Wis.)
DS351.5.K39   2003
958.1—dc21   2002075787

Printed in Malaysia

1 2 3 4 5 6 7 8 9 07 06 05 04 03

Contents

AN OVERVIEW OF AFGHANISTAN

Characterized by steep, snowy mountains, deep valleys, barren plateaus, and windy deserts, the Islamic State of Afghanistan is a landlocked country in south-central Asia. The nation has a long, tumultuous history dating back more than five thousand years. Throughout the centuries, Afghanistan's location often made it the battleground on which empires pursued their quest for regional control. Today, the country is recovering from decades of war, internal strife, and, more recently, life under the harsh Taliban regime. With the support of the international community, Afghanistan is now on the road to rebuilding itself as a stable, unified, and democratic nation.

Opposite: **The two giant Buddhas of Bamian were carved into the mountains north of the town more than 1,500 years ago. The statues were destroyed by the Taliban in March 2001.**

Below: **These young children are washing cooking utensils in a stream located next to their village in the region of Wakhan.**

THE FLAG OF AFGHANISTAN

The current flag of Afghanistan was adopted on January 27, 2002. The flag has three vertical stripes of black, red, and green. The emblem in the center of the flag features a mosque containing a *mehrab* (MEH-rahb), an arch in a mosque that indicates the direction of Mecca, and a *menber* (MUHN-brr), a many-tiered pulpit. The mosque in the emblem is flanked by two flags and encircled by two sheaves of wheat. At the top of the emblem is the inscription "There is no God but Allah, and Muhammad is His messenger."

Geography

With an area of about 250,000 square miles (647,500 square kilometers), Afghanistan is completely landlocked. The country is bordered by Uzbekistan and Tajikistan to the north, China to the northeast, Pakistan to the east and south, Iran to the west, and Turkmenistan to the northwest. The nearest coast is the Arabian Sea, which is about 300 miles (483 kilometers) to the south.

Mountains, Plateaus, Plains, and Deserts

High mountains cover much of Afghanistan. The Hindu Kush Range extends from the northeastern part of the country in a southwesterly direction. The mountains that make up the western part of this range gradually descend in height and fan out toward the city of Herat. The country's highest point, Nowshak Peak, at 24,558 feet (7,485 meters), lies in the northeastern part of the Hindu Kush Range, on the Afghan-Pakistani border.

The formidable Hindu Kush and its subsidiary ranges divide the country into three geographic regions: the Central Highlands, the Northern Plains, and the Southwestern Plateau. Including the Hindu Kush, the Central Highlands cover about 160,000 sq miles (414,400 square km). High mountains and deep valleys characterize this region.

SHAPED LIKE A LEAF

Afghanistan is roughly shaped like a leaf, with the region of Wakhan, in the northeastern part of the country, forming the stem.

DEVASTATING EARTHQUAKES

Approximately fifty earthquakes strike Afghanistan each year, with most occurring in the Hindu Kush. This mountainous area lies near the boundary of the colliding Eurasian and Indian tectonic plates. The collision of these plates shaped the region's rugged terrain and high mountains and continues to cause the frequent earthquakes that hit the area. In March 2002, a series of earthquakes measuring over 6 on the Richter scale destroyed several towns in the Hindu Kush region and killed about two thousand people.

Left: The province of Bamian is made up of deep valleys between the Hindu Kush and Koh-e-Baba mountain ranges.

Left: Flowing through the provinces of Konduz, Baghlan, and Bamian, the Konduz River is a major tributary of the Amu Darya River.

ENVIRONMENTAL ISSUES

Afghanistan is facing a crippling environmental disaster caused in part by years of warfare.
(A Closer Look, page 48)

The Northern Plains are located north of the Central Highlands. This area consists of plains and fertile foothills that stretch toward the Amu Darya River. The Northern Plains contain the nation's most productive agricultural land and, as a result, are densely populated.

Made up of high plateaus and deserts, the Southwestern Plateau is located south of the Central Highlands. The Registan Desert covers one-fourth of this region.

Afghanistan's Rivers

Helmand River is the longest river entirely within Afghanistan. With a length of 715 miles (1,150 km), the river flows southward from its source in the Koh-e-Baba Mountains. Amu Darya River originates in the Pamirs in the northeastern part of the country. The river forms a natural border between Afghanistan, Tajikistan, and Uzbekistan before emptying into the Aral Sea in Uzbekistan. Rising in central Afghanistan, the Harirud River flows west and northwest to the Iranian border before crossing into Turkmenistan. Kabul River is the main river in the eastern part of the country; this river flows east into neighboring Pakistan.

MOUNTAIN PASSES

Because Afghanistan's steep terrain makes traveling difficult, narrow passes, or pathways, through the mountains are of great military and economic significance. They have provided trade and invasion routes between Central Asia and the Indian subcontinent. The most famous pass is the Khyber Pass, which links Afghanistan and Pakistan. Other important passes include Salang Pass and Shebar Pass.

Left: **Mountains in the Hindu Kush Range lie to the north of the city of Kabul. The Afghan winter brings heavy snow to the nation's mountainous areas, and most of the country's water supply comes from this snow.**

Climate

Afghanistan's climate is characterized by severe winters and hot summers. The country, however, experiences regional climatic variations. The mountainous regions in the northeastern part of the country have a subarctic climate, while the southern mountainous areas that border Pakistan are affected by the Indian monsoons between July and September. These winds bring maritime tropical air and rain to the region.

Temperatures throughout Afghanistan vary according to elevation. Summer temperatures can reach 120° Fahrenheit (49° Celsius) in Jalalabad, one of the nation's hottest areas, while temperatures rarely exceed 90° F (32° C) in Kabul. In the Southwestern Plateau, temperatures average 95° F (35° C) during the summer months. Strong summer winds in this region are usually accompanied by intense heat, drought, and sandstorms. In winter, icy northern winds sweep over the country. Temperatures drop to 5° F (-15° C) and below in the high mountainous areas. The lowest temperature recorded at Kabul was -24° F (-31° C).

Annual rainfall in Afghanistan varies from less than 3 inches (8 centimeters) in the dry, western province of Farah to 53 inches (135 cm) in the Salang Pass in the Hindu Kush Range. Much of the country's precipitation falls in the form of snow between December and March. The Northern Plains and Central Highlands have deep snow all winter.

SEASONAL CHANGES

Spring in Afghanistan arrives by March 21, the Afghan New Year. In May, the country's orchards are in bloom, and wild flowers cover the hillsides. By mid-June, however, vegetation is burned away as the full heat of summer takes over. Autumn is the most anticipated time of year, as it is bright, clear, and cool, making it an ideal time for harvesting. The country's brutal winter is largely due to the cold air masses that sweep into the country from the north and northwest, bringing snowfall and freezing temperatures.

Plants and Animals

Afghanistan's once abundant plant and animal life has been significantly reduced due to war and environmental problems. Pine and fir trees can be found in the nation's high mountains. At lower elevations, oak, walnut, alder, ash, and juniper trees grow. Many trees, however, have been cut down for fuel, and, as a result, forests now cover about 10 percent of Afghanistan. Dominated by sandy deserts and dry regions, the southern part of the country has very little vegetation.

The mountains and foothills provide homes for a wide variety of animals, such as wolves, jackals, foxes, and striped hyenas. These areas are also home to a number of endangered species, including snow leopards. Wild goats and ibexes are found in the Pamirs, while wild sheep live in the Pamirs and the Hindu Kush Range.

Bird life is abundant in Afghanistan. About four hundred and sixty species of birds can be found in Afghanistan, of which more than two hundred breed in the nation. Partridges, ducks, and pheasants abound, while birds of prey include eagles and vultures. Many of these species, however, are becoming increasingly rare.

AFGHAN HOUND

A type of dog that has long been found in northern Afghanistan, the Afghan hound is used predominantly as a hunting dog. With a height of 24 to 28 inches (61 to 71 cm) and weighing between 50 and 60 pounds (23 and 27 kilograms), the Afghan hound has a reputation for being a fast runner and strong jumper, making it extremely valuable in Afghanistan's mountainous terrain. The tall, elegant hound also has floppy ears and a long, silky coat.

AN IMPORTANT MIGRATORY ROUTE

During spring and autumn, many bird species make Afghanistan their temporary home while migrating between Siberia and Pakistan. One bird species whose traditional migratory path takes it over Afghanistan is the Siberian crane, which is globally endangered. Constant fighting in the nation in recent years, however, has led many migratory bird species to fly alternative paths.

Left: A camel herder looks on as young camels graze on the green pastures of central Afghanistan.

History

Early human life in Afghanistan can be traced back as far as 100,000 years ago. Archaeologists believe that the region north of the Hindu Kush was one of the first to be settled by people who engaged in agriculture. About 2,000 B.C., a nomadic group called the Aryans moved into the area from Central Asia.

Dynasties, Empires, and Kingdoms

The Achaemenids of southern Persia (now Iran) conquered much of present-day Afghanistan in the sixth century B.C. Alexander the Great overthrew the Achaemenids before crossing into modern-day Pakistan in 327 B.C. Following Alexander's death in 323 B.C., several kingdoms vied for control. Land south of the Hindu Kush fell to the Mauryan Empire of northern India in 304 B.C., while the Seleucid Dynasty ruled Bactria (now Balkh).

In 135 B.C., five Central Asian nomadic tribes gained control of Bactria, bringing the religion of Buddhism with them. The Kushans emerged as the dominant tribe, and, under their rule, the tribes conquered the rest of Afghanistan. Under the Kushan Dynasty, the arts, religion, and trade flourished. After the decline of the dynasty, invaders fought for control of territories.

THE BUDDHA STATUES OF BAMIAN

Part of the Afghan landscape since the fifth century A.D., the two giant Buddhas at Bamian (*above*) made headline news in March 2001 when the two ancient statues were destroyed by the Taliban. (*A Closer Look, page 44*)

Left: This illustration shows Alexander the Great (356 B.C.–323 B.C.) mounted on his horse, Bucephalus. Alexander was responsible for introducing Greek culture to the countries he invaded, including Afghanistan.

Left: **One of the most famous conquerors of history, Genghis Khan invaded the area now known as Afghanistan in the thirteenth century, making it part of his huge empire that stretched from China to the Adriatic Sea in Europe.**

The Arrival of Islam

In the seventh century A.D., Arabic armies invaded Afghanistan, bringing the religion of Islam with them. Following the armies' departure, those they converted to Islam returned to their old beliefs. By the eleventh century, however, King Mahmud of the Ghaznavid Dynasty had firmly established Islam throughout the area. Mahmud consolidated and expanded the dynasty's territorial boundaries considerably and also promoted the arts, literature, and architecture. The Ghaznavid Dynasty gradually declined after Mahmud's death.

In 1150, the Ghurid Dynasty rose to prominence but was defeated by the Khwarezm-Shah Dynasty in the early thirteenth century. In 1219, the Mongol conqueror Genghis Khan invaded Afghanistan and devastated the land. Following Genghis Khan's death in 1227, local chiefs either established independent states or acknowledged Mongol princes as their sovereigns. At the end of the fourteenth century, however, Timur, another Mongol conqueror, invaded the country, and most of the country fell under the control of the Timurids. Under their rule, the arts and architecture flourished, and the nation enjoyed peace and prosperity for a hundred years.

Throughout the sixteenth and seventeenth centuries, the rulers of the Mughal Empire and those of the Safavid Dynasty in Persia battled each other for control of Afghanistan.

THE EMERGENCE OF THE MUGHAL EMPIRE

In 1504, Turk Zahir-ud-Din Muhammad Babur, a descendant of Genghis Khan and Timur, took control of Kabul. With the aim of expanding his territory into India, Babur conquered Kandahar in 1522 and Delhi, the center of the Delhi Sultanate (a Muslim territory that included northern India), four years later. The takeover of Delhi marked the beginning of the Mughal Empire, which included the eastern part of Afghanistan south of the Hindu Kush. Throughout their rule, which lasted until the mid-nineteenth century, successive Mughal rulers strove to retain Kabul and Kandahar from the Persian Safavid Dynasty. The Persians eventually gained Kandahar in the early seventeenth century.

International Rivalry

In 1709, the Hotakis (a branch of the Pashtun tribe) revolted against their Persian ruler and, by 1722, had invaded Persia. Persian Nader Qoli Beg defeated the Hotakis and, in 1736, became shah, or king, of Persia. He extended his rule westward as far as Delhi. After Nader Shah's assassination in 1747, a tribal council in Kandahar elected Ahmad Khan Abdali as the shah.

In the nineteenth century, Afghanistan became the focal point of international conflict due to its geographical location. The Anglo-Russian rivalry known as the Great Game led to two wars. After the Second Anglo-Afghan War (1878–1880), the British gained control of Afghanistan's foreign affairs.

In 1880, 'Abdur Rahman Khan became emir, or ruler, of Afghanistan. During his reign, the British and the Russians established the borders of what became present-day Afghanistan. As a result, Afghanistan became a buffer between the British and Russian empires. 'Abdur Rahman consolidated his power throughout the territory by suppressing numerous internal revolts. He also developed a strong central government and began industrializing the economy. 'Abdur Rahman was succeeded by his son, Habibullah I, without dispute in 1901.

After Habibullah I was assassinated in 1919, his son Amanullah seized power and led Afghanistan into the Third Anglo-Afghan War. The Treaty of Rawalpindi, which was signed

THE DURRANI DYNASTY

After his election as shah, Ahmad Khan Abdali established the Durrani Dynasty. Ahmad Shah enjoyed the support of most Afghan tribal leaders, headed a central government, and had full control of domestic and foreign affairs. At its peak, the empire stretched from Meshed (now Mashhad, Iran) in Persia to Delhi, India, and from the Amu Darya River to the Arabian Sea. The empire began to disintegrate after 1798, and its territories were gradually reduced.

THE GREAT GAME

Rivalry between the expanding British and Russian empires greatly affected Afghanistan in the 1800s. By then, the British controlled the Indian subcontinent, while the Russians held the Central Asian lands to the north. British concerns over Russian advances in Central Asia and Russia's growing influence in Persia led to the First Anglo-Afghan War between 1839 and 1840. The Second Anglo-Afghan War took place from 1878 to 1880.

Left: Persian and British politicians meet in Kabul in 1880.

Left: Afghan prime minister Mohammad Daud Khan (*left*) is greeted by Yugoslavian president Tito (*right*) at Belgrade Airport, Yugoslavia, in August 1961.

on August 8, 1919, ended the one-month-long war and forced the British to relinquish control of Afghanistan's foreign affairs.

From Absolute Monarchy to a Republic

After establishing Afghanistan's independence, Amanullah set about modernizing the country. His reforms, however, offended religious and ethnic leaders, and civil war broke out in 1928. Amanullah fled the country the following year. A tribal assembly elected Mohammed Nader Khan as shah. He was assassinated in 1933 and was succeeded by his son Mohammad Zahir.

The modernization of Afghanistan continued during Zahir Shah's reign, and the country prospered. In 1964, Zahir Shah adopted a new constitution that established a constitutional monarchy. In the early 1970s, drought and famine ravaged the country. Lieutenant General Mohammad Daud Khan, Zahir Shah's cousin and prime minister from 1953 to 1963, took advantage of the situation and, in 1973, overthrew the king in a coup d'état. He declared Afghanistan a republic with himself as prime minister. Daud Khan's attempts to introduce urgently needed economic and social reforms were largely futile, and the 1977 constitution failed to end political instability. In 1978, Daud Khan was killed in a leftist military coup.

THE PEOPLE'S DEMOCRATIC PARTY OF AFGHANISTAN

Zahir Shah's 1964 reforms allowed the emergence and growth of unofficial extremist parties on both the left and right. These parties included the People's Democratic Party of Afghanistan (PDPA). A communist party, the PDPA had close ties to the Soviet Union. In 1967, the PDPA split into two rival factions. Noor Mohammad Taraki and Hafizullah Amin headed the Khalq faction and had support within the military, while the Parcham faction was led by Babrak Karmal. This split reflected ethnic and ideological divisions within the Afghan people. These factions of the PDPA, however, joined forces to overthrow Daud Khan's government in 1978.

(A Closer Look, page 62)

MOHAMMAD ZAHIR SHAH

Afghanistan's last king, Mohammad Zahir Shah, ruled the country from 1933 to 1973. After living in exile for almost thirty years, Zahir Shah finally returned to Afghanistan on April 18, 2002. On this day, Afghans, including these soldiers (*left*), marched through the streets of Kabul to celebrate the return of the former king.
(A Closer Look, page 62)

External Intervention and Internal Strife

Following the 1978 coup, Noor Mohammad Taraki became president. The government's reform programs angered many Afghans, and revolts sprang up all over the country. Conflicts within the PDPA also surfaced, and Hafizullah Amin overthrew Taraki to become president. Alarmed by Amin's inability to suppress the continued nationwide revolts, the Soviet Union invaded Afghanistan in December 1979 and installed Babrak Karmal as president. The new government was unpopular, and fighting broke out between Soviet forces and Afghan guerrillas. After ten years of warfare, the Soviet Union withdrew its troops from Afghanistan. The civil war, however, continued. In 1992, a power struggle between mujahedin factions led to the election of Burhanuddin Rabbani as president. Fighting between rival groups intensified, and, in 1994, the Taliban emerged as the dominant group. By the late 1990s, the Taliban ruled almost all of the country, while opposition forces referred to as the Northern Alliance and supported by Rabbani held only a small part of northern Afghanistan. Following the terrorist attacks against the United States in September 2001 and the Taliban's refusal to surrender the prime suspect in the attacks, Saudi Arabian militant Osama bin Laden, the Taliban regime was overthrown in late 2001 by the Northern Alliance and the U.S.-led coalition against terrorism.

THE SOVIET INVASION

On December 24, 1979, Soviet troops crossed the border into Afghanistan, sparking a decade-long war that left over one million people dead and led between five and six million Afghans to flee their homeland.
(A Closer Look, page 66)

MUJAHEDIN

During the Soviet-Afghan War, a number of groups, collectively known as the mujahedin, emerged throughout Afghanistan, as well as in neighboring Pakistan, to fight the Soviet troops. These guerrillas had in-depth knowledge of Afghanistan's mountainous terrain and received financial and military backing from the United States, Saudi Arabia, Iran, and China.
(A Closer Look, page 64)

Meena Kishwar Kamal (1957–1987)

Born in Kabul, Meena Kishwar Kamal founded the Revolutionary Association of the Women of Afghanistan (RAWA), a group that strives for equal rights for Afghan women, peace, freedom, and democracy in Afghanistan, in 1977. Meena worked hard to promote RAWA, and she strongly criticized the Soviet-backed Afghan government and the Soviet occupation of Afghanistan. She was killed in 1987 in Quetta, Pakistan, allegedly by Afghan agents of the KGB, the secret police force of the former Soviet Union.

Amanullah Khan (1892–1960)

The son of Habibullah I, Amanullah Khan seized control of the throne following the assassination of his father in 1919. Striving to end British control over Afghanistan's foreign affairs, he initiated the Third Anglo-Afghan War in 1919, which led to Afghanistan's independence. In 1923, Amanullah changed his title from emir to king. He then initiated a series of reforms aimed at social and political modernization. These moves angered many ethnic and religious leaders and caused political turmoil. In 1928, civil war broke out, and Amanullah abdicated on January 14, 1929. He died in exile in 1960.

Amanullah Khan

Mohammad Daud Khan (1909–1978)

Lieutenant General Mohammad Daud Khan became the prime minister of Afghanistan in 1953. As prime minister, Daud Khan accepted military and economic aid from both the United States and the Soviet Union. He also introduced educational and social reforms. His support for the creation of a Pashtun state in the Afghan-Pakistani border area increased tensions with Pakistan and led to his resignation in March 1963. A decade later, Daud Khan seized power in a military coup. He abolished the monarchy and declared Afghanistan a republic with himself as prime minister. Daud Khan tried to decrease the country's reliance on Soviet aid. In 1977, he became president and appointed relatives and friends to the government. This move sparked widespread demonstrations throughout the country and angered factions within the PDPA. A year later, Daud Khan and most of his family were killed during a PDPA-led coup.

Mohammad Daud Khan

Government and the Economy

Following the defeat of the Taliban regime at the end of 2001, the United Nations (U.N.) set about establishing a broad-based, multiethnic, and fully representative government in Afghanistan. The first major step was taken in November 2001, when representatives from Afghanistan's major ethnic, religious, and political factions — excluding the Taliban — met in Bonn, Germany, to discuss the country's political future. The Bonn Agreement that emerged put in place an interim government that led Afghanistan for six months. Established on December 22, 2001, the interim government was to eventually consist of the Afghanistan Interim Administration (AIA), the Supreme Court, and a special independent commission. The main task of the interim government was to establish an emergency *loya jirga* (LOY-ah jir-GAH). In June 2002, the emergency loya jirga elected Hamid Karzai to be the head of state, whose responsibility is to lead Afghanistan's transitional government for the next eighteen months. By 2004, nationwide elections are expected to be held and a new constitution adopted.

LOYA JIRGA

A unique Afghan institution meaning "grand assembly," a loya jirga enables ethnic elders, including Pashtuns, Tajiks, Hazaras, and Uzbeks, to come together to settle affairs of the country. The loya jirga is the only political process accepted by all of Afghanistan's ethnic and religious groups and is regarded by many as the only way to select a representative government that is recognized by all the Afghan people. The emergency loya jirga established in 2002 consisted of over fifteen hundred members.

Left: Between November 27 and December 5, 2001, representatives from four major Afghan factions and U.N. representatives attended the U.N. Talks on Afghanistan in Bonn, Germany. During the conference, the four Afghan factions agreed to the creation of an interim administration that would pave the way for a more permanent transitional government.

Left: AIA chairman Hamid Karzai speaks at a press conference held at the Presidential Palace in Kabul, in March 2002.

The Afghanistan Interim Administration

The AIA held power from December 2001 to June 2002. Headed by Hamid Karzai, a Pashtun tribal leader, the interim administration consisted of thirty members. Members of the AIA represented Pashtun, Tajik, Hazara, and Uzbek communities, as well as the country's other ethnic groups. In addition, two women held positions in the administration. The AIA was responsible for the country's internal and external affairs.

The Special Independent Commission

Established on February 7, 2002, the special independent commission consisted of twenty members (seventeen men and three women), most of whom were professors. The purpose of the commission was to determine the number of representatives in the loya jirga, as well as the procedures within the loya jirga. The loya jirga, in turn, formulated the structure of Afghanistan's transitional government.

The Judicial System

Afghanistan's judicial system is independent and vested in the Supreme Court, which administers lower courts at provincial, municipal, and district levels. The AIA established a judicial commission to rebuild the country's judicial system in accordance with Islamic principles.

A HISTORY OF CONSTITUTIONS

Since 1923, Afghanistan has had five constitutions. The 1923 and 1931 constitutions gave the monarchy absolute power. The 1964 constitution provided for a constitutional monarchy, with separate executive, legislative, and judicial branches. In 1977, a new constitution was passed, but it was superseded in 1987 by another new constitution, which was amended in 1990. In 1992, the Soviet-backed communist government fell, but agreement over a new constitution remained deadlocked due to persistent fighting between numerous rival mujahedin groups.

HARSH BUT BRIEF: LIFE UNDER THE TALIBAN

From 1996 to late 2001, Afghanistan was under the rule of the ultra-conservative group called the Taliban. The Taliban changed the name of the country to the Islamic Emirate of Afghanistan and imposed strict Islamic law. Mullah Muhammad Omar was named head of state, and all government positions were held by Islamic religious leaders.
(A Closer Look, page 52)

Economy

Since 1979, Afghanistan has faced immense economic problems. The Soviet military occupation and the subsequent civil war led to serious food and fuel shortages, industrial collapse, severe damage to the country's infrastructure, and high inflation. As a result, Afghanistan today is one of the poorest countries in the world.

Agriculture dominates the Afghan economy and employs 70 percent of the workforce. Only about 6 percent of the country's total land area, however, is under cultivation. Farming methods are primitive, and the use of machines, chemical fertilizers, and pesticides is uncommon. Wheat is the nation's chief crop and the staple food of the Afghan people. Other grains grown include barley, corn, and rice. Cotton is another widely cultivated crop. Fruits, such as grapes, apricots, and figs, and nuts are among the country's most important exports. Animals also play a vital role in Afghanistan's agricultural economy. Various types of sheep are raised in large numbers; goats, camels, and donkeys are also kept. Since 1999, Afghanistan has been devastated by severe drought. Crop production has halved, and farmers' livestocks

Above: **These young Afghans are fishing in a river in the province of Bamian. The country's rivers, lakes, and streams have a wide variety of freshwater fish, but their numbers are limited.**

Opposite: **This fruit and vegetable seller sells fresh produce at a market in the city of Kandahar.**

have been heavily depleted. As a result, millions of people in Afghanistan face famine and starvation.

Afghanistan has a wealth of natural resources. Exploitation of these resources, however, has been hampered by internal strife, the country's remote and rugged terrain, and an inadequate transportation system. Natural gas is the nation's most important resource. About ninety percent of Afghanistan's natural gas output was exported to the Soviet Union, but this ended after the Soviet withdrawal in 1989. Other minerals found in the country include iron ore, copper, coal, and lapis lazuli, a semiprecious stone.

Afghanistan's industrial sector is in shambles. Most of the nation's factories have been destroyed during the decades of fighting. Cotton-textile production is the most important of the country's industries. Other industries in Afghanistan include cement, sugar, vegetable oil, and woolen textiles.

Irrigation

Agricultural production relies heavily on irrigation. For centuries, the country's plains and valleys have been sustained by hundreds of miles (km) of irrigation channels, known as *karez* (CAH-rahz), that deliver water to low-lying areas. Most of this system of tunnels, trenches, and wells sunk deep into the nation's mountains, however, is drying up due to the crippling drought that has hit the country or has been destroyed by war.

TRANSPORTATION

Afghanistan's poor transportation system has further hampered the country's struggling economy. Most roads are in a state of disrepair, and the highway network is in need of almost total reconstruction. A stretch of the Amu Darya River is the country's main waterway; the rest of the nation's rivers are virtually unnavigable. Public transportation in urban areas consists of buses and colorfully painted trucks (*above*), but most city dwellers travel on foot or ride bicycles. For rural Afghans, the main means of transportation are walking or riding on donkeys, horses, and sometimes camels. Afghanistan has forty-six airports, including international airports at Kabul and Kandahar, but most of the nation's airport facilities have been destroyed during the years of warfare.

People and Lifestyle

As Afghanistan is located at the crossroads of many civilizations, its population represents a mix of ethnicities and languages. Although the Afghan people are related to many of the ethnic groups in Iran, Pakistan, Tajikistan, Turkmenistan, and Uzbekistan, the country's main ethnic groups are the Pashtuns, Tajiks, Hazaras, and Uzbeks. The diverse population of Afghanistan has contributed to the country's rich cultural traditions, but it is also the root of many of Afghanistan's social, political, and ethnic tensions.

Most Pashtuns live in southern and eastern Afghanistan. Making up about two-fifths of the population, the Pashtuns have traditionally been the nation's dominant ethnic group and have a strong tribal organization. The Pashtuns are divided into tribes, the most important of which are the Durranis and the Ghilzays. The Durranis have traditionally been the most politically influential group in the country. Most Pashtuns are employed in the agricultural sector, although some are nomads.

The Tajiks are the country's second-largest ethnic group. Descendants of various ancient Iranian, Turkic, and Mongol peoples, most Tajiks live in the provinces of Badakhshan, Herat, and Kabol. They are farmers, merchants, and skilled artisans.

FLEEING THEIR HOMES

After the Soviet invasion and occupation of Afghanistan and the subsequent civil war of the 1990s, many Afghans fled the country and became refugees in neighboring nations, most notably Iran and Pakistan. Today, an estimated 1.5 million Afghan refugees can be found in Iran, and more than two million Afghan refugees are believed to live in refugee camps in Pakistan. The actual figures, however, may even be much higher. During the internal strife of the 1990s, when extensive fighting broke out in the countryside, many Afghans also fled their homes in rural areas to seek refuge in Kabul, the country's capital city. This trend, however, had reversed by the end of the 1990s as people fled Kabul back to the country's rural areas to avoid bombing and constant fighting within the city. Today, many rural residents, such as these young children and their families (*left*), are moving closer to the country's cities, including Kabul, because international aid is distributed from these locations.

THE KOCHIS

Following a centuries-long tradition of migrating between mountain peaks and desert steppes, the Kochis, or nomads, of Afghanistan (*left*) make up a sizable percentage of the country's population. Following years of war and drought, however, the traditional lifestyle of the Kochis is threatened.
(A Closer Look, page 58)

The Hazaras predominate in central Afghanistan. Believed to be descended from Mongols who first invaded the country in the thirteenth century, most Hazaras are sheepherders and farmers.

The region north of the Hindu Kush is home to a number of ethnic groups who speak Turkic languages. The Uzbeks form the largest of these groups. Once nomads, the Uzbeks now engage in agriculture and trade. Both the Kyrgyz, who live in the remote northeastern region of Wakhan, and the Turkmens are mainly seminomadic herdsmen.

Several smaller ethnic groups are scattered throughout the country. The Baluch, a seminomadic tribal people, live in the far southern part of the country and engage in seasonal farming and livestock raising. While most Nuristanis make their home in the province of Nuristan, some are known to live in the provinces of Laghman and Nangarhar. The Chahar Aimaks are concentrated mainly in the western part of the central mountain region.

KABUL

During the city's long history, Kabul was famous for its gardens, bazaars, mosques, and magnificent palaces. Today, most of the city has been reduced to rubble by years of bitter fighting.
(A Closer Look, page 54)

Family Life

Although the Afghan population is made up of different ethnic groups, their living patterns are essentially the same. The family is the center of Afghan society. Consisting of several generations, the family is strongly male-oriented and is headed by the oldest man of the household.

Afghans usually do not choose their spouses. Parents still arrange most marriages. A match between paternal cousins is preferred because the union strengthens family ties. When Afghan women marry, they become members of their husband's family. Traditionally, women run the household and raise the children, while the men are responsible for the family's agricultural or business activities.

Pashtunwali

Primarily belonging to the Pashtuns, the unwritten laws and codes of *pashtunwali* (PASH-tuhn-wah-lee) are followed by most Afghans. The system revolves around a code of honor, courage, and self-pride. Hospitality is extremely important as it enables individuals to uphold personal and family honor. Therefore, food, drink, and shelter are available to all who seek it. Afghans must also avenge any insult made against themselves, their families, or their tribe. Consequently, some feuds can run from generation to generation.

HEALTH

Chronic health problems brought on by war, political instability, economic hardship, and severe drought plague Afghanistan. Life expectancies are among the lowest in the world, and 25 percent of children die before their fifth birthday. Leading causes of childhood death include diseases, such as measles, malaria, and pneumonia. Lack of safe drinking water and malnutrition also contribute to the nation's severe health problems.

At present, the country's health system is one of the poorest in the world. Health-care facilities lack basic equipment and are in urgent need of restoration. With a critical shortage of health-care workers, it has been estimated that there is only one doctor for every fifty thousand Afghans.

Rural Life

Most Afghans live in rural villages that are scattered from the mountains in the north to the deserts in the south. Each family lives in a mud-brick house or a compound containing a cluster of houses. The house or compound is surrounded by high mud walls that provide security from enemies, seclusion for women, and a pen for livestock. Most houses have flat roofs on which people sleep in summer to keep cool. Each village has a leader who is chosen by the other male members of the village. The country's kochis, or nomads, follow similar living arrangements except they live in tents rather than houses. Most rural areas do not have access to basic infrastructure, such as running water, electricity, and clean drinking water.

Urban Life

The majority of Afghanistan's urban population lives in the country's main cities. Although well-to-do families live in houses with gardens that are surrounded by high walls, most city dwellers live in high-rise buildings. After the country's years of warfare, most buildings and essential infrastructure, including water, sewage, and telecommunications systems, have been damaged or destroyed by artillery fire and bombs.

WOMEN IN AFGHANISTAN

In a country where female illiteracy is high and many women have never visited a doctor, much needs to be done to improve the overall well-being of the millions of Afghan women.
(A Closer Look, page 70)

Below: **These men in the province of Bamian are trying to rebuild their lives by constructing a new home for their family.**

Left: **This majestic mosque is located in Kabul.**

Religion

Islam is the official religion of Afghanistan. Ninety-nine percent of the Afghan population is Muslim. Eighty-four percent of the population belongs to the Sunni branch of Islam, while 15 percent are Shi'ite.

All Muslims believe in one God — Allah — and believe that Muhammad was his prophet. The differences in belief between Sunni and Shi'ite Muslims arose after the death of Muhammad and continue to divide the two branches today. Shi'ites regard Muhammad's direct descendants as the only legitimate leaders of the Islamic world. Sunni Muslims, however, accept other claims to leadership. Among Afghanistan's ethnic groups, Pashtuns, Tajiks, Uzbeks, and Turkmens are predominantly Sunni Muslims, while most Hazaras are Shi'ites.

The Five Pillars

The Islamic faith has five principles, known as the Five Pillars of Islam, that every Muslim should follow. The first principle is the declaration of faith a Muslim performs by reciting, "There is no God but Allah, and Muhammad is His messenger." The second is to pray to Allah five times a day. The third principle involves

MAZAR-E SHARIF

Home to a gold- and blue-tiled mosque and shrine where Hazrat Ali is believed to be buried, Mazar-e Sharif is a leading place of Muslim pilgrimage.
(A Closer Look, page 60)

donating money to the poor and needy. The fourth principle involves fasting during daylight hours for one month during the Islamic holy month of *Ramazan*, (RAM-ah-ZAHN), or Ramadan. The fifth principle is for every Muslim to make a pilgrimage to the holy city of Mecca, in Saudi Arabia, once in his or her lifetime.

Mullahs and Mosques

Mullahs are important figures in Muslim life in Afghanistan. Mullahs teach the principles of Islam, lead prayers in mosques, instruct children and adults in religious schools, and conduct weddings and funerals. In addition, mullahs act as judges and counselors, offering advice and solutions to social and personal problems.

Mosques not only serve as places of worship, they are also communal meeting places. After Friday prayers, people usually stay at their local mosque to meet distant relatives and friends and to chat and exchange news. Mosques also provide shelter for guests and are the focal point of social and religious festivities.

Left: **These Afghan women are praying outside the Blue Mosque in the city of Mazar-e Sharif.**

Language and Literature

Over thirty languages and dialects are spoken in Afghanistan, reflecting the ethnic diversity of the Afghan people. Dari, which is a form of Persian, and Pashto, however, are the country's official languages. Fifty percent of the population, including Tajiks and Hazaras, speak Dari, while Pashto is the language of the Pashtuns. Although most educated Afghans can speak Dari and Pashto, Dari is the language in which business is most frequently conducted. Both Dari and Pashto are written using adaptations of the Arabic alphabet. Turkic languages are spoken by 11 percent of the population, including Uzbeks and Turkmens. Various other languages and dialects of major languages are spoken by smaller ethnic groups in Afghanistan. Bilingualism is very common.

Left: **Afghan men read books and magazines that are on sale at a roadside stall in central Kabul. Among the most popular newspapers in Kabul are the Dari-language newspaper** *Anis,* **the Pashto-language daily** *Hewaad,* **and the English-language** *Kabul Times.*

Literature

Afghanistan has a rich literary tradition that stems from the works of poets, historians, and philosophers who began writing in Persian in the ninth century. Poetry has been the most popular literary medium among Afghans, and the country has produced many eminent poets. Throughout the centuries, popular themes in Afghan poetry have been war, love, jealousy, religion, and folklore. The thirteenth-century poet Maulana Jalaluddin Balkhi Rumi (1207–1273) is a world-renowned Dari poet whose works were based on his deep Islamic beliefs and cultural evaluations. The works of poets such as Khushal Khan Khattak (1613–1690) and Rahman Baba (1651–1710) helped develop Pashto literature considerably in the seventeenth century. Widely regarded today as the country's national poet, Khattak used verse to express pashtunwali, the tribal laws and codes of Pashtuns. He also wrote poetry about war, love, and everyday life. Contemporary Dari prose and poetry, such as the works of Ustad Khalilullah Khalili (1907–1987), often imitate classical Persian style and form.

Modern Afghan literature also deals with freedom and the destruction of the country by war. Since writers within Afghanistan are struggling to survive everyday life, most works about the Soviet occupation and life in refugee camps have been written by Afghans living abroad.

USTAD KHALILULLAH KHALILI

Regarded as Afghanistan's greatest Dari poet of modern time, Ustad Khalilullah Khalili was born in Kabul in 1907. Khalili was extremely interested in literature, particularly poetry, and studied classical literature with Islamic scholars. During the reign of Zahir Shah, Khalili held a number of government positions. After the 1978 coup, he went into exile in neighboring Pakistan, where he wrote poetry that mourned the fate of the Afghan people and encouraged them in their struggle to defeat the occupying Soviet troops. By the time of his death in 1987, Khalili's works were widely read by the Afghan population.

Arts

Afghanistan's arts reflect the country's historical roots and its location as a crossroads for diverse ethnic groups and traditions. Although the Afghan people have been drastically affected by warfare, their arts have continued to flourish.

Architecture

Afghanistan is home to many architectural feats that reflect the country's eclectic past. Excavations stretching from the Khyber Pass to the province of Balkh have uncovered Buddhist stupas and monasteries that date back to the nation's Buddhist era. By the eleventh century, however, Islamic architecture predominated. As this style of architecture developed, architects combined Persian and local styles to create magnificent and awe-inspiring buildings and mosques. Afghanistan's beautiful mosques are characterized by tall minarets, domes, and colorful, intricate tilework. Considered by many as the nation's greatest works of art, some of Afghanistan's most impressive mosques include the Friday Mosque in Herat and the Blue Mosque in Mazar-e Sharif.

Calligraphy

Calligraphy, the art of elegant handwriting, has flourished in Afghanistan for centuries. Calligraphic inscriptions are used in abundance to decorate mosques, buildings, and everyday objects, such as plates and vases. Calligraphic inscriptions are usually poems or verses from the Koran.

Handicrafts

Afghanistan is renowned for its brightly colored woven carpets. Typically made of wool, the carpets are hand knotted by women and girls. Carpet styles differ according to ethnic group and region. Turkmen and Uzbeki carpets characteristically have parallel rows of geometric figures on a dark red background. The Baluch, well-known producers of prayer rugs, also make carpets mainly of wool, using a blend of dark colors. Afghans excel at other forms of arts and crafts, including embroidery, pottery, gold and silver jewelry making, and metalworking.

Above: **This man is restoring a calligraphic inscription on the inside wall of a building in the city of Kabul.**

TRADITIONAL CLOTHES

Traditional Afghan dress has similarities to traditional clothes worn in neighboring countries, such as Pakistan. Although Afghans throughout the country tend to wear similar styles of dress, differences in costumes can help identify a person's native region or his or her ethnic group.
(A Closer Look, page 68)

Opposite: **This Afghan trader in the northern city of Konduz is arranging an array of handicrafts and pottery to sell at his shop.**

Folk Dances

Afghanistan's diverse ethnic groups perform an amazing array of energetic folk dances that help preserve their historical and ethnic ties. Intricate step patterns, quick turns of the wrist, and frequent spins are essential to Afghan dancing.

Originating in the Pashtun areas of the country, the *attan* (AH-tan) is the country's national dance. This warlike dance is performed by male Afghans. Standing in a large circle, the dancers clap their hands and quicken the movements of their feet to the beat of the music. The attan is performed on special occasions, such as religious festivals and weddings. Afghanistan also boasts many regional dances. One such dance, which is known as logari, comes from the eastern province of Logar. This dance is performed to music with a fast beat and frequent pauses. The skilled dancer must stop with the music and hold her pose until the music starts again. Women also perform intricate, expressive forms of dance. These dances require the female dancers to tell a story that depicts everyday female activities using expressions and hand movements.

Music

Afghanistan has a rich, diverse musical heritage ranging from folk music to pop music, all of which blends styles and rhythms originating from the cultures of various peoples known to

Left: **A Pashtun man dances to the beat of traditional Afghan drums in the southern part of Afghanistan. Traditional folk dances play a major role in Afghanistan's cultural life, as this form of entertainment helps preserve historical and ethnic roots.**

Left: **This young Kyrgyz girl is playing a wooden lute outside her family's hut in the region of Wakhan in the northeastern part of Afghanistan.**

Afghanistan and its neighbors. A wide variety of instruments are used to play traditional Afghan music. The national instrument of Afghanistan, the *rubab* (ruh-BAHB) is similar to a banjo. It is played by plucking the strings and creates short, fast sounds. The *tanbur* (TAN-bur), a long-necked lute, and the *dutar* (DEW-tar), a fourteen-stringed lute, are often used to perform regional folk music. Another popular instrument is the harmonium. The harmonium resembles an organ and has hand-pumped bellows. The musician plays the keyboard with the right hand, while the left hand pumps the bellows. Afghan musicians also play a variety of drums, which they beat using their palms and fingers. The *dowl* (DOWL) is one such instrument, and its deep thumping sounds provide an infectious beat for Afghan melodies.

Popular Afghan musicians include Ahmad Zahir, Ustad Mawash, Ahmad Wali, and Nashenas, while Nainawas and Ustad Sarahang are well-known Afghan composers.

AHMAD ZAHIR

Regarded as one of Afghanistan's greatest singers, Ahmad Zahir entertained Afghan audiences with his unique combination of Western and Eastern musical styles and mesmerizing lyrics.
(A Closer Look, page 72)

Leisure and Festivals

Most forms of entertainment were banned during the years of Taliban rule. Although traditional Afghan leisure activites are now making a comeback following the establishment of the new government, most opportunities for leisure and entertainment are limited, as Afghans struggle to survive the hardships of everyday life.

Traditionally, singing and dancing are popular forms of entertainment for most Afghans. Both men and women dance, although not together. Card games, such as bridge, and chess are also common leisure activities for Afghan adults.

Afghan men spend time in teahouses where they drink tea, talk, and listen to music. They also engage in more violent leisure activities, such as animal fighting. Cocks and partridges are most commonly used, and fights continue until one of the birds tires. Betting is common at these events.

Children's Games

Afghan children play local variations of games such as hide-and-seek, tag, and blindman's bluff. *Bujul-bazi* (buh-JULL-bah-ZEE) is also extremely popular. This game resembles marbles but is played with sheep's knuckles.

THE GREAT STORYTELLERS

The ancient art of storytelling continues to flourish in Afghanistan. This age-old practice of telling folktales through the spoken word is a highly developed and much appreciated art form. Folktales cover all areas of Afghan life and often teach traditional values, beliefs, and behavior. These stories are also a major form of entertainment in Afghanistan.
(A Closer Look, page 50)

Left: Two Afghan men play a game of chess outside a shop in the city of Kabul. Chess is played all over Afghanistan and is a popular way for men to spend their free time. Due to the competitive nature of most Afghans, chess games can turn into daylong matches.

KITE FLYING

Kite flying is a popular pastime among Afghan boys and men. The sky above cities and rural areas is often filled with soaring flashes of color that dance in the wind.

(A Closer Look, page 56)

Girls enjoy playing a number of games, including a game similar to hopscotch. They often will play by imitating their mothers at work. This type of role-playing is good training because girls usually start to help their mothers at an early age. Girls also can entertain themselves for days playing a memory game that involves a chicken wishbone. Two girls break the wishbone in half, and each keeps one half. They then try to trick each other into looking at their half of the wishbone. When one girls succeeds, she shouts, "Memory for me, forgetfulness for you!" As they get older, Afghan girls learn to embroider and become very skilled at decorating their own clothes, scarves, and dolls with beautiful designs.

Egg fighting and pigeon playing are typically boys' sports. In egg fighting, each player has a hard-boiled egg. One player holds his egg tightly while his opponent bumps his own egg into the other player's egg, hoping to crack it. The winner of the game is the owner of the uncracked egg. Although it may sound simple, this game has a technique and strategy behind it. As boys grow up, they graduate from egg fighting to pigeon playing. Many boys keep flocks of pigeons in special houses and release them for exercise. Other boys try to lure away released pigeons with calls or whistles or trap the birds in nets. The boys either return the captured birds to the owner, sell them, or keep them.

FAMILY PICNICS

Going on a picnic is a favorite Afghan pastime, particularly during the spring and autumn months. Families take a picnic and sit in fields, gardens, or parks where they eat and drink. Storytelling, dancing, and socializing are common. Before war broke out, the city of Jalalabad, known for its vast, lush gardens, was a popular spot for picnicking, and some families would travel for hours to reach there.

Festivals

Afghanistan celebrates many religious festivals that follow the Islamic lunar calendar. Other holidays mark age-old traditions or reflect the Afghan people's historical struggle to free the nation from external intervention.

Religious Festivals

The most important month of the Islamic calendar is Ramazan, also known as Ramadan, the Islamic month of fasting. During this time, healthy adult Muslims should not eat, drink, or smoke during daylight hours. Following the sighting of the new moon, *Eid al-Fitr* (EED AHL-fitr), a three-day festival, celebrates the end of Ramazan. After going to the mosque in the morning to pray, Afghans visit relatives and friends and entertain guests. *Eid al-Adha* (EED AHL-ad-ah), the Feast of the Sacrifice, falls in the last month of the Islamic year. Commemorating Abraham's willingness to sacrifice his only son to God, this festival is celebrated with the sacrificing of goats and sheep.

To Afghanistan's Shi'ite Muslims, the first ten days of the new year are extremely important. This is a period of mourning that commemorates the martyrdom of Husain, the grandson of Muhammad. Many Shi'ites choose to fast on the tenth day of this month.

Left: **Muslims pray at the Jamae Mosque in the western city of Herat on the first day of Ramazan in November 2001.**

National Holidays

The celebration of Afghanistan's national holidays was banned under the Taliban regime. *Nawruz* (NOW-rooz), the country's most important secular celebration, however, was reinstated in 2002. Deeply rooted in the traditions of Zoroastrianism, the religion of ancient Persia, Nawruz, which falls on March 21, marks the arrival of spring. Preparations for the holiday begin weeks in advance, with spring-cleaning and the making of new clothes for the family. Special foods also are prepared, including *samanak* (SAH-MAN-ak), a dessert made of wheat and sugar, and *haft-mehwah* (HAFT-MAY-wah), a mixture of seven fruits and nuts that symbolizes spring. Festivities include large family picnics, fairs, and carnivals. On this day, many pilgrims flock to the tomb of Hazrat Ali at the Blue Mosque in Mazar-e Sharif.

Other holidays that were banned under the Taliban regime include Labor Day on May 1, Remembrance Day for the Martyrs and the Disabled on May 4, and Independence Day on August 19. Independence Day celebrates the end of Britain's control over Afghan foreign affairs and Afghanistan's establishment as an independent nation.

Above: Afghans lift a flag pole and flag in Kabul's Ziarat-i-Sakhi Ali Square on March 21, 2002, as part of the festivities to celebrate Nawruz, the Afghan New Year. The 2002 Nawruz celebrations were particularly significant for the Afghan people as the festival had been banned under the former Taliban regime.

Food

Although traditional Afghan food mixes all the cuisines of the people who have settled in the country throughout the centuries, the strongest influences are from Iran, India, and Pakistan. Like Iranian cuisine, Afghan food includes a wide variety of soups, rice dishes, and kabobs while using the spices and rich sauces common in Indian and Pakistani dishes.

Rice and a flatbread known as nan usually form the basis of any Afghan meal. Other basic foods include cheese, chicken, lamb, eggs, and fruits. Afghans use an amazing array of spices and seasonings to flavor their food, including saffron, pepper, cardamom, coriander, cumin, dill, and mint.

Rice is prepared in a variety of ways. It can either be served plain or with meat, herbs, and sauces. Red rice is flavored with pomegranate juice and yellow rice with saffron or shredded

EATING CUSTOMS

Afghan Muslims follow a set of dietary laws that are prescribed by Islam. Pork is not eaten because this type of meat is considered unclean.

Afghans eat their meals sitting cross-legged on the floor around a large cloth or rug. They wash their hands before and after eating. Afghans generally eat using their right hand, although some Afghans living in urban areas use cutlery.

DROUGHT AND FAMINE

Following the severe drought that has affected Afghanistan since 1999, the country has faced grave food shortages. Because the lack of rain has prevented the successful harvesting of crops, millions of Afghans now are dependent on food aid distributed by international aid agencies.

Left: A variety of fruits is on sale in a market in the western city of Herat. Herat is well known for its fruits, especially grapes, that are grown on the fertile plains surrounding the city.

FRUITS AND SWEET DESSERTS

Fruits, such as melons, grapes, pomegranates, and apricots, frequently are served by Afghans. They also prepare rich, sweet desserts, including a milky pudding with almonds and cardamom and deep-fried dough that is covered with thick, sweet syrup.

BEVERAGES

Tea is the most popular drink in Afghanistan. Black tea is popular south of the Hindu Kush, while green tea is preferred by Afghans living north of the mountains. Afghans often prepare green tea with cardamom. Both types of tea are served after meals (*below*) and at the country's many teahouses. Another favorite drink is *dogh* (DOUGH), which is made from yogurt.

orange peel. In *sabzi challow* (saab-ZEE cha-LOW), a dish cooked traditionally to celebrate Nawroz, spinach and chunks of lamb are added to the rice before being grilled. *Quabili pallow* (KAH-bih-lee pah-LOW) is by far the most popular rice dish in Afghanistan. Usually prepared for guests, this baked rice dish consists of lamb or chicken and onions garnished with sautéed carrot slices, raisins, pistachios, and almonds.

Rice dishes are complemented with meat and vegetables. Kormas, or thick vegetable pastes containing small pieces of meat, are common, and eggplant, bell peppers, potatoes, and pumpkin are sautéed and served with yogurt sauces. A finely chopped salad made of onions, tomatoes, coriander, cucumbers, and lemon juice is also a favorite side dish.

Noodles and pastas are also popular in Afghan cuisine. *Aush* (AHSH) is a traditional soup made with noodles, yogurt, kidney beans, and chickpeas that is flavored with dill, turmeric, and mint. *Aushak* (AHSH-ak) is crescent-shaped ravioli filled with leeks and onions and topped with yogurt, mint, and a meat sauce.

Consisting of small cubes of meat skewered with onions and tomatoes, kabobs are popular among Afghans. There are many different varieties of kabobs, all of which are marinated in herbs and spices and charbroiled on skewers. Other favorite foods include battered and fried vegetables and fried pastries filled with potatoes, leeks, eggplant, and beef.

A CLOSER LOOK AT AFGHANISTAN

In the last decades of the twentieth century, Afghanistan was associated with war, mujahedin guerrillas, drought, and the Taliban. Indeed, due to its strategic geographical location, the country and its people have suffered greatly throughout history. Nevertheless, the nation has enjoyed some periods of relative stability and peace, most recently during the reign of Mohammad Zahir Shah. Since the 1978 coup, however, Afghanistan has known nothing but warfare and the misery that comes with it. The country was at war with the Soviet Union for ten years and then descended into the worst civil war it has ever experienced.

Opposite: **A man riding a donkey leads camels carrying loads past a mosque that has been partially destroyed in the province of Balkh.**

Emerging as the strongest faction during the civil war, the Taliban took control of most of the country and inflicted an ultraconservative form of Islam on its people.

Despite years of conflict, hardship, and Taliban regulations, Afghans have kept their rich cultural heritage alive. They enjoy watching and playing buzkashi, flying kites, and listening to the music of popular singers. The country, however, is struggling to overcome troubling environmental issues and to rebuild its cities, including Kabul and Mazar-e Sharif.

Above: **After years of conflict, these Afghans in the central province of Bamian yearn for a brighter future in a peaceful Afghanistan.**

The Buddha Statues of Bamian

At the Crossroads of Civilizations

In ancient times, central Afghanistan, including Bamian, was strategically placed along the Silk Road. The Silk Road was an ancient trade route that linked China and the West. Silk from China and wool, gold, and silver from the West were transported and traded along the route. During this time, Buddhism spread throughout Afghanistan, and Buddhist statues, stupas, and monasteries soon were built all over the country.

Ancient Wonders of the Silk Road

In the fifth century A.D., two magnificent Buddha statues were carved out of the cliffs north of the town of Bamian. The larger statue stood 175 feet (53 m) high, while the smaller one was 120 feet (37 m) tall. Both statues are believed to once have been decorated with gold, jewels, and colored paints. Grouped around the statues was a series of humanmade caves.

Below: Located northwest of Kabul, the town of Bamian lies at an elevation of 8,495 feet (2,590 m). The two giant Buddhas and the ancient man-made caves were carved into the cliffs north of the town more than 1,500 years ago.

Left: The Buddha statues at Bamian were regarded among Afghanistan's most important and well-loved monuments. The larger of the two was the tallest Buddha in the world. In March 2001, the Taliban used explosives to blow up the statues' legs and cause extensive damage to their bodies and heads.

Gone But Not Forgotten

The great Buddhas survived the wars and foreign invasions that troubled Afghanistan over the centuries. In the autumn of 1998, however, the town of Bamian fell into the hands of the Taliban. As strict followers of Islam, the Taliban showed little, if any, tolerance for statues, including pre-Islamic figures, that depicted human or animal representations. The Taliban viewed all these statues as non-Islamic. Despite their ban on idols and non-Islamic images, Taliban officials originally assured the international community that the Bamian statues would not be harmed.

This assurance turned out to be an empty promise. At the beginning of 2001, Taliban supreme leader Mullah Mohammad Omar ordered the systematic destruction of all the country's non-Islamic statues, including the Buddha statues at Bamian. Despite heavy protest from around the world, the Taliban dynamited the two Buddhas in March 2001 as part of its campaign to eradicate all traces of Afghanistan's non-Islamic heritage.

FIGHTING A LOSING BATTLE?

Many countries, including Islamic nations, and international organizations appealed to the Taliban against the destruction of the two Buddhas at Bamian. Fearing the loss of the statues, both India and New York City's Metropolitan Museum of Art offered to transfer the two Buddhas for safekeeping, but the Taliban rejected these proposals. Even after the destruction of the Buddhas, the Taliban refused Sri Lanka's offer to buy the remains of the statues in the hope of reconstructing them. The Buddhas, however, may not be lost forever. The United Nations Educational, Scientific, and Cultural Organization (UNESCO) is now looking into the possibility of reconstructing the great Buddhas of Bamian.

Buzkashi

The ancient game of buzkashi has been played in northern Afghanistan for centuries and is now enjoyed throughout the country. The Dari word *buzkash*i means "goat pulling," and the sport reflects the boldness and fierce competitive spirit of the Afghan people.

A Competitive Game

Although different variations of the game exist, the most popular forms of buzkashi are *tudabarai* (TOO-dee-bah-REE) and *qarajai* (CAH-rah-JYE). Both of these versions start with the carcass of a goat or calf, which weighs up to 150 pounds (68 kg), placed in the center of a circle. The riders, who are divided into two teams, then surround the circle. The object of the game is for one member of a team to get control of the carcass and carry it to the scoring area. In tudabarai, the rider must grab the carcass and then carry it away from the starting circle in any direction to gain points. In qarajai, however, the task is more complex. The player must carry the carcass around a marker and return it to the team's designated scoring circle. Competition is fierce, and the winner of the game receives prizes that range from money to clothes.

Left: Spectators sit on top of vehicles to watch a game of buzkashi in northern Afghanistan. The great equestrian tradition from which buzkashi developed dates back to the time of Genghis Khan.

Left: These two riders are fighting for possession of the carcass during a game of buzkashi in the city of Mazar-e Sharif. Buzkashi is a dangerous sport, but intensive training and excellent communication between the rider and horse help minimize the risk of injury. Buzkashi horses are trained vigorously and possess special qualities. For instance, when a rider falls off his horse, the horse will wait for him to remount. In addition, a well-trained horse will gallop as soon as its rider snatches the carcass to get away from opposing players.

The Horsemen and the Horses

During buzkashi, only the most masterful players, known as *chapandaz* (cha-PAN-dawz), get close to the carcass. Riders train for years to gain the skills of a chapandaz, and the best players are often over the age of forty. Chapandaz have to be able to perform a feat of balancing while pulling, pushing, snatching, and carrying away the carcass to deposit it in the designated area.

The players are not the only ones who undergo extensive training. The horses that are used in buzkashi are trained for five years before they can be ridden in a buzkashi game.

Part of the Afghan Way of Life

To many Afghans, buzkashi is not just a game, it is a way of life — a way in which teamwork and communication are essential to being successful. During the years of Taliban rule, the game was rarely played, but now the sport is experiencing a comeback. Traditionally, Afghans play buzkashi on special occasions such as at the start of the new year or at weddings.

Environmental Issues

More than two decades of war have plunged Afghanistan into an environmental crisis. About 10 percent of the nation remains forested, as trees have been chopped down to burn for cooking and heat. In addition, rivers and irrigation canals are drying up, and land mines and cluster bombs litter the countryside.

Deforestation

Deforestation, or the destruction of forests, is probably the most serious environmental problem facing Afghanistan. As many of the nation's power plants and electrical lines have been destroyed, most Afghan families depend primarily on wood from the country's few remaining forests as fuel for heating and cooking purposes. In addition to local demand, trees are being cut down and transported across the border for sale in Pakistan.

As trees are cut down, the rich topsoil, which had been protected by tree roots, is either being blown away by the wind or washed by the rain into nearby tributaries or rivers, leaving behind bare and barren land. Experts believe that all Afghanistan's land eventually will be unfit for even the most basic form of agriculture.

Left: **This Afghan man is unloading firewood to be sold at a market in the city of Konduz in northern Afghanistan. Due to the high demand for wood both within and outside Afghanistan, environmentalists fear all of the country's forests will disappear by 2005.**

Inadequate Water Supplies

Another major environmental concern is the lack of clean water. The destruction of many of the country's irrigation systems and the lack of precipitation over the past few years have strained Afghanistan's water supplies. Today, many of the country's rivers, streams, and wells have dried up, and the remaining water supplies have been contaminated by human and animal waste. The lack of clean water and sanitation creates conditions for cholera and dysentery. However, people have little choice but to drink from these contaminated sources.

Above: **This Afghan soldier is searching for land mines in the fields surrounding the city of Jalalabad in eastern Afghanistan.**

Land Mines and Cluster Bombs

Years of war and the recent U.S.-led air campaign have left millions of land mines and cluster bombs scattered throughout the country. These explosive devices have destroyed essential irrigation systems, caused loss of productive agricultural land, and inflicted significant suffering on human and animal populations. Furthermore, land mines and cluster bombs introduce poisonous substances into the environment as their casings erode. The decomposition of these substances can cause many environmental problems because the substances are often water soluble, toxic, and long lasting.

Afghanistan is one of the most heavily land mined countries in the world. Planted by all factions in Afghanistan's civil and guerrilla wars, an estimated ten million land mines lie hidden all over the nation. Land mines explode when someone steps on them or when a field is plowed. The mines are designed to maim adult victims, but when children step on them or play with them unknowingly, the mines are powerful enough to kill. It has been estimated that land mines kill twenty to thirty Afghans each day. Land mines also threaten the survival of the Afghan people because they render much of the nation's farmland unusable.

Cluster bombs are usually dropped from military aircraft or fired from rocket launchers on the ground, and each cluster bomb contains about two hundred smaller, independent bomb units, or "bomblets," which would be liberally peppered over an area measuring approximately 53,820 square feet (5,000 sq m). Bomblets have a high initial failure rate, which means that they do not always explode on first contact. Packed with tiny steel shards, bomblets are more devastating than land mines.

The Great Storytellers

Afghans are skilled storytellers. Children spend hours gathered around the family members who are most well known for creative and detailed stories. The best storytellers usually are grandparents, who are affectionately referred to as *bebejan* (BEE-BEE-jawn), or "my sweet dear," or *baba-kalan* (BAH-bah-KAH-lawn), meaning "older father."

Stories for very young children feature rhymes, repetition, and sounds. These stories are similar to nursery rhymes that contain short plots and some singing parts. Tales for older children usually contain morals and teach them how to be good Muslims. Afghans also have been known to use storytelling as a way to scare their children from venturing too far from the family home or getting in trouble.

Popular Afghan Characters

Traditional Afghan tales often center around main characters. Kal Bacha, or Bald Boy, is one such character. Kal Bacha is the youngest and most mischievous of several brothers. The tales of Bald Boy include a story in which he fails at his first village job and another in which he marries a beautiful princess.

Left: **Children all over Afghanistan love to gather around older family members, most notably their grandparents, to hear stories about their favorite Afghan heroes and heroines.**

Stories of heroic warriors and doomed lovers are also popular with Afghans. The tragic love story of Leila and Majnun is one of the most famous, and many different versions are told. In one version of the tale, the two childhood friends fall in love but are not allowed to marry. They separate, and when they finally meet again, they realize that they have grown apart and no longer have anything in common. The story of Malalai is a favorite among Afghan girls. Malalai became a heroine for her courage and valor when she carried the Afghan flag into battle against British soldiers in 1880.

Above: **Everyday activities, such as visiting an outside barber, provide ideal opportunities for Afghans to exchange stories.**

The Jin

One strange creature found in Afghan folklore is the *jin* (JIN). Jins are described either as invisible or as troll-like. Jins are usually blamed for sudden noises, flickering lights, and awkward silences. Many Afghans believe that various types of jins exist. Superstitious Afghans say a jin has entered a person when he or she becomes angry or irrational.

SHAH-NAMEH

One poem popular among Afghans is the epic *Shah-nameh*, or *The Book of Kings*. Completed in 1010 by poet Ferdowsi (c. 935–c. 1020–26), the poem describes in rhymed verse the history, legends, and myths of the kings of pre-Islamic Persia.

Harsh But Brief: Life Under the Taliban

As the Taliban gained control of major cities and towns throughout Afghanistan in late 1994 and 1995, they restored peace, stamped out corruption, and allowed trade to flourish again. Consequently, they were welcomed by many Afghans who were weary of the prevailing lawlessness in most parts of the country. When the Taliban finally captured Kabul, the capital city, in 1996, most Afghans hoped life would return to normal under the new regime. This return to normality, however, never emerged. The Taliban ruled with an iron fist for the next five years.

Strict Laws

The Taliban's ultimate aim was to make Afghanistan the purest Islamic state in the world. By imposing what many regarded as an extreme interpretation of Islam, the Taliban attracted widespread international criticism for repeatedly committing human rights violations, notably against women and girls.

TIGHTENING THEIR GRASP

In 1997, the Taliban issued an edict that renamed the country the Islamic Emirate of Afghanistan and installed their leader, Mullah Mohammad Omar, as head of state and Commander of the Faithful. This meant that Mullah Omar held complete power. The Taliban also introduced a strict form of Shari'a, or Islamic law. The Taliban's judicial system was made up of a Supreme Court in Kabul, two levels of courts (local and high) in the provinces, and special religious courts. The Taliban used the courts to further strengthen their hold over the Afghan population. Punishments handed down by the courts were based on the edicts of Taliban officials.

Left: Taliban ambassador to Pakistan Abdul Salam Zaeef (*left*) and deputy ambassador to Pakistan Sohail Shaheen (*right*) exchange words while holding a press conference inside the Afghan embassy in Islamabad, Pakistan, on October 22, 2001.

Within days of gaining power, the Taliban began to enforce their rules on the Afghan people. All forms of entertainment were banned, including music and dancing. Movie theaters and television stations were shut down, and works of art that depicted the images of humans or animals were destroyed. Men were ordered to grow full, untrimmed beards. Women were forbidden to appear in public without wearing *chadaris* (CHA-dah-REES), garments that covered them from head to toe, and had to be accompanied by a male relative. Women who were considered improperly dressed were beaten. Girls' schools were closed, and women were no longer allowed to work outside the home. In addition, women were only allowed to receive medical care in female-only clinics of which there were very few.

Throughout their rule, the Taliban continued to impose additional rules and laws daily. These laws and rules were announced over the radio by the government-owned radio station, Radio Kabul, and from trucks equipped with loudspeakers. Murder, adultery, and drug dealing became punishable by death, and public stonings were also allowed. Other rules imposed by the Taliban included the punishment of theft by amputation.

All of the Taliban's rules and laws were rigidly enforced by the religious police, a wing of the Ministry for the Promotion of Virtue and Prevention of Vice.

A LARGELY UNRECOGNIZED REGIME

During their five-year rule, the Taliban failed to achieve the international recognition they sought. Most countries did not recognize the Taliban regime as the legitimate government of Afghanistan. Only the Islamic governments of Pakistan, Saudi Arabia, and the United Arab Emirates acknowledged the legitimacy of the Taliban. By the end of the Taliban's rule, however, only Pakistan officially recognized them as the government of Afghanistan. Most countries spurned the Taliban because of their infringements on human rights. In addition, the Taliban regime was widely criticized for harboring the Saudi Arabian militant Osama bin Laden, who lived in Afghanistan as a guest of the Taliban government from the mid-1990s until their overthrow. The Taliban were believed to have been financially and politically supported by bin Laden.

Kabul

Lying at an elevation of about 5,900 feet (1,800 m), Kabul is the largest city in Afghanistan. Also the country's capital city since 1776, Kabul is the nation's chief economic and cultural center. Once boasting an eclectic mix of old and modern architecture, much of the city has been reduced to rubble by the years of civil war.

A Turbulent Past

As invading nations and factions within the country have fought for control of the city, the history of Kabul has been one of destruction and rebuilding for more than three thousand years. First rising to prominence in the eighth century, much of Kabul was destroyed by Mongol conqueror Genghis Khan in the thirteenth century. The city was made into the capital of the Mughal Empire by Turk Zahir-ud-Din Muhammad Babur in 1504. Although the empire's capital was moved to Delhi, India, in 1526, Kabul remained an important Mughal center until the city was captured by Persian ruler Nader Shah in 1738.

In 1979, Kabul was occupied by the Soviet Union. The withdrawal of Soviet troops in 1989 propelled Kabul and the rest of the nation into the worst civil war that the country had ever

A STRATEGIC CITY

Located in east-central Afghanistan, Kabul has long been of strategic importance because of its location near Kabul River and its proximity to the Khyber Pass, an important mountain pass that leads to Pakistan.

KABUL'S POPULATION

During the fighting that took place between 1992 and 1996, about thirty thousand inhabitants of Kabul are believed to have lost their lives. Today, about 2.6 million people live in the Kabul area. Tajiks are the main ethnic group living in the city, but the Pashtuns are an important minority.

Left: Male inhabitants of Kabul walk down one of the streets of the capital city before U.S. military operations began in late 2001. The hustle and bustle of city life can still be experienced in areas of Kabul, notably around the city's bazaars.

experienced. With the collapse of the communist government in 1992, Kabul fell into the hands of the mujahedin. As these forces divided into rival warring factions, the city and its inhabitants suffered increasingly. The Taliban seized control of the city in 1996, and it remained one of their strongholds until November 2001.

A City in Ruins

Following the years of fighting, there is a dire need for reconstruction to improve living conditions in Kabul. Most of the city lacks access to basic infrastructure, such as running water, electricity, and clean drinking water. Public buildings, businesses, and homes lie in ruins, and roads and telecommunication systems are also in shambles.

Nevertheless, Kabul is home to some historical and cultural sites that have survived the ravages of war. Located in the old section of the city, Babur's Garden, which includes the emperor's tomb, was a popular spot for Afghans before the war. With artifacts dating back to pre-Islamic times, Kabul Museum once housed the most comprehensive record of Central Asian history. During the early 1990s, the building was damaged by shells and gunfire, and most of the museum's treasures were plundered.

KABUL UNIVERSITY

Founded in 1946, Kabul University was once regarded as one of the finest institutions in Central Asia and was the intellectual heart of the country. The university, however, was shut down when civil war broke out in 1992. Kabul University has been partially opened again but needs much reconstruction to be able to operate normally.

Kite Flying

Known as *gudiparan bazi* (GOO-dee-PAH-RON bah-ZEE) in Dari, kite flying is a popular sport in Afghanistan. Kite flying is now making a comeback throughout the country after being banned by the Taliban regime. A predominantly male pastime, Afghan kite flying and kite fighting call for physical and technical skill as well as a competitive nature.

Kite Making

Afghan fighter kites are made from thin tissue paper and a bamboo frame. Kites come in various sizes. The smallest is about 10 to 12 inches (25.4 to 30 cm) in width, while the largest can reach 5 feet (1.5 m).

Vital to successful kite fighting is the *tar* (TAHR), or line, that is attached to the kite. Afghan kite flyers coat the kite tar with ground glass to make it sharp. Making this glass-coated "cutting" line requires skill and patience, and most kite flyers make their own, using secret recipes of glue and ground glass. Typically, they crush glass and, then, mix the ground glass with glue and soak the tar in the mixture. The tar is then pulled out

Left: **Young Afghans gather enthusiastically at a shop in the southern city of Kandahar to buy kites. Kite fighting tournaments usually are held on Fridays after Afghans have been to the mosque to pray. Large, flat fields throughout the country make excellent kite fighting arenas.**

Left: **An Afghan boy launches his colorful kite from a rooftop in the city of Kabul. A skilled kite flyer knows how to maneuver his kite and can make it swoop strategically.**

of the mixture and left to dry overnight. Once dried, the tar is tough and jagged. Some creative kite flyers mix color into their glue mixtures to help them distinguish their line when in flight.

Kite Fighting

Two kites have to be airborne and close together for a fight to take place. The aim of the fight is to cross lines with another kite fighter and then use a sawing motion to sever the opponent's kite line, thus cutting loose the other kite. The fight begins as soon as the kites' lines have made contact and can last from a second to an hour.

The length of the match depends on a number of factors, including the direction and strength of the wind, the difference in quality of lines, and the experience and patience of the fighters. Children get very excited when a kite is cut, and they often chase after the kite until it lands. The child who finds the kite gets to keep it.

Soaring High

Skilled kite fighters are experts in understanding wind patterns by the way the line tugs and slips through their fingers. They know just when to feed the line out and when to haul it in again.

VICTORY!

The general belief among Afghan kite fighters is that the kite line should be released and not pulled during a fight. The faster the fighter releases the line, the more likely he is to win the airborne fight.

The Kochis

For centuries, Afghan Kochis, or nomads, have migrated annually along traditional routes between Afghanistan and Pakistan. A proud and resilient people who number around 2.5 million, Kochis keep alive one of the world's most difficult ways of life.

On the Move

Moving from place to place, these wandering people are always looking for grazing grounds for their livestock, which normally consists of camels, donkeys, cattle, sheep, and goats. The Kochis are mainly Pashtuns, but there are also a small number of Turkmen Kochis. Each autumn, these nomads descend from the highlands of southern Afghanistan with their livestock and cross the border into southern Pakistan. In summer, they return to Afghanistan, herding their livestock toward grazing pastures in the southern part of the country.

Kochis primarily travel in the early hours of the morning when the heat from the sun is not so intense. When traveling, Kochis walk in a line behind their livestock. Camels and donkeys carry the traveling Kochis' bundled necessities, which include tents, sleeping mats, cooking pots and utensils, bags of grains, and dried dung, which is used as cooking fuel.

Below: **These Kochis have set up camp next to a stream in the highlands of southern Afghanistan.**

KOCHI CLOTHING

Kochi men (*left*) wear long tunics, baggy trousers, and turbans. Kochi women are known for their distinctive dress. They usually wear colorful, long-sleeved dresses and cover their head and shoulders with a long shawl. Some women wear bright red trousers. Kochi women are skilled embroiderers, and they adorn their clothes with ornamental bands of silver coins and small mirrors in geometric shapes. They also wear heavy jewelry around their necks, wrists, and ankles.

Setting up Camp

After a day of traveling, the men unload the animals and pitch the tents, while the women collect water and cook. Whenever possible, Kochis pitch their tents near running streams. Pashtun Kochis live in large black tents that are usually made of goat skin, while Turkmen Kochis live in red-domed tents. Kochi tents have strong wooden frames that can be disassembled quickly. The Kochis depend heavily on the milk products, meat, wool, and skins of their flocks for food and clothing.

The End of the Road?

More than two decades of warfare, the three-year drought, and the presence of ten million land mines throughout the country have taken a huge toll on the Kochis. As their nomadic way of life is becoming increasingly difficult, many Kochis are being forced to abandon their traditional lifestyle. According to U.N. officials, groups of Kochis are now settling in camps on the edges of Kandahar and other cities in the hope of receiving desperately needed humanitarian aid. While international aid agencies acknowledge that the Kochis' need for aid is great, the agencies fear the Kochis will settle in one place, and, as a result, their nomadic ancient way of life will be lost forever.

DEPLETING FLOCKS

Twice a year, Kochis pass through villages that are located on their migratory routes. Villagers traditionally allowed the Kochis to graze their animals on their lands. The nomads bought supplies, such as wheat, from the villagers, while the villagers bought wool, hides, and milk products from the Kochis. Following the devastating droughts that have hit Afghanistan, however, it has become increasingly difficult for Kochis to find grazing pastures. As a result, most of the nomads' animals have starved, and the Kochis have few, if any, trading products.

Mazar-e Sharif

The capital of Balkh province in northern Afghanistan, Mazar-e Sharif lies just south of the border with Uzbekistan and about 200 miles (322 km) northwest of Kabul, the capital city. Mazar-e Sharif has long been one of Afghanistan's main trading centers. The city is located in one of the most fertile regions of the country, and the main products of the area include cotton, grain, and a variety of fruits. The city's industries include flour milling and the manufacturing of exquisite silk and cotton textiles. The population of Mazar-e Sharif is mainly Uzbek, Tajik, and Turkmen.

A Key City

Due to its proximity to the Uzbekistan border, Mazar-e Sharif has been a key city in times of war. After the Soviet invasion in 1979, Soviet forces set up a military command in the city and built a road and rail bridge north of Mazar-e Sharif across Amu Darya River to the border town of Termiz in Uzbekistan, which was then a Soviet republic. The Soviets used the bridge to transport military supplies into Afghanistan during the Soviet-Afghan War.

By 1996, after the Taliban had taken control of much of Afghanistan, Mazar-e Sharif remained a stronghold of opposition

Left: **These Afghan women and children are gathered outside the Blue Mosque in the city of Mazar-e Sharif.**

groups. Between May and July 1997, the Taliban attempted to capture the city but failed. They eventually succeeded in ousting opposition forces in August 1998. The Taliban controlled the city until it was recaptured, in November 2001, by the Northern Alliance with the help of the U.S.-led coalition against terrorism.

Above: With its amazing blue- and gold-tiled walls, the Blue Mosque in the northern city of Mazar-e Sharif is a wonderful example of Islamic architecture.

The Blue Mosque

Mazar-e Sharif, which means "tomb of the saint," is most famous for the blue- and gold-tiled mosque and shrine that mark the location of the tomb where Hazrat Ali, the cousin and son-in-law of the prophet Muhammad, is believed to be buried. The site is revered by Muslims, especially Shi'ite Muslims, and thousands make pilgrimages to the city each year. The pilgrims bring offerings and make vows and contributions in Hazrat Ali's name. In return, they hope Hazrat Ali's spirit will, for example, heal a sick family member or protect their family's property. Afghans from all over the country also flood to the city on Nawruz, which is a widely celebrated festival in Afghanistan, to witness the raising of a green-and-pink flag at the mosque. The flag-raising ceremony marks the beginning of spring and the arrival of the new year.

THE MASSACRES OF MAZAR-E SHARIF

During heavy fighting in Mazar-e Sharif in 1997, anti-Taliban forces killed at least two thousand Taliban soldiers. A year later, the Taliban captured the city and, according to human rights groups, killed up to four thousand people in retaliation.

Mohammad Zahir Shah

Mohammad Zahir Shah ruled Afghanistan for almost forty years. During his reign, Afghans enjoyed a long period of relative peace and stability, and the country was transformed into a constitutional monarchy, with a bicameral parliament, free elections, and universal suffrage.

A Period of Peace and Stability

Born in 1914, Zahir Shah became king of Afghanistan at the age of nineteen, following the assassination of his father, Mohammed Nader Shah, in November 1933. During the early years of his reign, power was exercised by Zahir Shah's uncles. In 1953, Lieutenant General Mohammad Daud Khan, the king's cousin, became prime minister and ran the government. Following Daud Khan's resignation in 1963, Zahir Shah began to assert his own authority.

In 1964, the king introduced a new constitution, which brought about the establishment of a parliament, free elections, and a free press. In addition, members of the royal family were prohibited from holding public office. Zahir Shah actively supported a number of social reforms, such as improving the status of women in Afghan society, and economic-development

Left: **During his reign, Zahir Shah realized the importance of maintaining friendly relations with other nations and, as a result, traveled to many countries to meet with other heads of state. Here, Zahir Shah is pictured with Britain's Queen Elizabeth II during a state visit to London in December 1971.**

Left: **On April 19, 2002, Zahir Shah (*left*) and interim leader Hamid Karzai (*center*) visited the tomb of the former king's father in the city of Kandahar. Zahir Shah returned to his homeland the day before after nearly thirty years in exile. He made it clear that he did not intend to reclaim the throne, and he supports Karzai and the country's current government.**

projects, which included irrigation and road construction. He also maintained Afghanistan's position of neutrality in international politics.

In the early 1970s, however, Afghanistan suffered a severe drought and famine, which worsened the country's economic conditions. In addition, Pashtun groups living along the border with Pakistan revived their demands for autonomy. While on a trip to Italy, the king was deposed in a bloodless coup on July 17, 1973. The coup was led by General Daud Khan who declared Afghanistan a republic with himself as head of state. Zahir Shah formally abdicated on August 24, 1973.

Ready to Return

Following his abdication, the former king lived in exile in Rome, Italy. Although he did not play an active role in Afghan politics for almost thirty years, Zahir Khan expressed his desire to return to Afghanistan to help establish a new government and restore democracy in his homeland following the fall of the Taliban in late 2001. Accompanied by interim leader Hamid Karzai, the former king returned to Afghanistan on April 18, 2002. The former king is viewed by many Afghans as a symbolic and unifying figure among the country's various ethnic groups.

Mujahedin

Known throughout the world for their resilience and fighting spirit, the mujahedin were the opposition groups that formed to fight against the Soviet occupation of Afghanistan between 1979 and 1989. Although the various factions cooperated during the war, they battled each other in the civil war that engulfed the country after the Soviet withdrawal.

A Resistance Movement is Born

The mujahedin movement was born following the installation of the Soviet-backed Afghan government and the subsequent Soviet invasion of Afghanistan in December 1979. The word *mujahedin* means "holy warriors." These anticommunist rebel fighters regarded the Soviet invasion not only as a threat to Afghanistan's independence but also to their religion of Islam. Consequently, the rebels declared a jihad, or holy war, against their invaders, and the word *mujahedin* soon came to define the whole rebel movement in Afghanistan.

Having grown up in Afghanistan, the mujahedin guerrillas were able to climb the country's high mountains and survive in extreme weather conditions. Their understanding of the rugged

WHAT IS JIHAD?

Meaning "strive" or "struggle," the word *jihad* can be interpreted in different ways. For some Muslims, it represents the struggle to defend their faith and ideals against harmful outside influences. For others, it means the struggle to promote justice and the Islamic social system, as well as to rid the Islamic world of western influence in the form of oppressive leaders and occupying armies.

Left: **Mujahedin fighters protect their stronghold with military equipment supplied by the United States, China, Saudi Arabia, and Iran.**

Left: This mujahedin fighter poses for a photograph in the mountains of the Hindu Kush Range.

terrain helped them hide in caves and tunnels during Soviet attacks and launch their own mountainside offensives. By the early 1980s, the United States, Saudi Arabia, and Pakistan had begun to supply the rebels with military equipment. This external support changed the course of the war and helped the mujahedin improve their fighting tactics and organization. The rebels' determination finally paid off in 1989 when the final Soviet troops withdrew from Afghanistan, following the signing of an agreement known as the 1988 Geneva Accords. This victory earned the mujahedin worldwide recognition as relentless, patriotic warriors.

The Emergence of the Taliban

Peace, however, did not last long. A civil war soon broke out between the mujahedin factions and the government. This internal strife created and brought into power the Taliban, who held fundamentalist Islamic beliefs. Promoting themselves as a new force for peace, they quickly gained support among the Afghan population, notably Pashtuns. The Taliban came to power in 1996 and gradually took over about 90 percent of the country for the following five years.

THE TALIBAN

The Taliban were organized in 1994 by Mullah Mohammad Omar in the southern city of Kandahar. The name *Taliban* is the plural form of *talib* (TAH-lib), a Pashto word meaning "student." Consisting mainly of Pashtuns recruited from Koranic schools within Afghanistan and in the Afghan refugee camps in Pakistan, the Taliban aimed to dominate the central government in Kabul. The Taliban first made headline news in 1994 when they were appointed by the Pakistani government to protect a convoy trying to open up a trade route from Pakistan to Central Asia.

The Soviet Invasion

In 1979, troops from the Soviet Union invaded Afghanistan to help the Afghan communist government suppress anticommunist Muslim guerrillas. What many thought would be a short conflict lasted ten years, cost over one million lives, and subsequently propelled Afghanistan into its worst civil war.

Sowing the Seeds of War

In April 1978, left-wing military officers overthrew President Daud Khan and installed a communist government. The new government, which had close links with the Soviet Union, did not have much support among the Afghan people. Dissent among the country's ethnic groups grew, and they began to organize themselves into anticommunist groups that aimed to overthrow the government. This opposition, as well as internal fighting within the Afghan government, greatly alarmed the Soviet Union, which regarded Afghanistan as a new stronghold of communism. Consequently, Soviet forces invaded the country on December 24, 1979, with the goal of keeping the communists in power.

Below: **Soviet troops arrive in Kabul, Afghanistan's capital city, in January 1980, following the outbreak of the Soviet-Afghan War in December 1979.**

Left: Jubilant mujahedin fighters celebrate the capture of a Soviet tank in April 1980. Although the Soviets had superior weapons and complete air control, the Afghan rebels generally managed to elude Soviet attacks.

At War

After seizing Kabul, the Soviet Union installed Babrak Karmal, a staunch Afghan communist, as president. By this time, the Muslim rebel groups, or mujahedin as they were commonly known, had grown in size and were active throughout the country. The war soon settled into a stalemate. The number of Soviet troops, originally about thirty thousand, increased to more than a hundred thousand. These troops controlled Afghanistan's cities and large towns, while the mujahedin roamed the countryside.

The mujahedin rebels were supported by the United States and Saudi Arabia, both of which sent aid to the rebels via Pakistan. As the war progressed, the organization and tactics of the rebels improved, and they eventually were able to neutralize Soviet air power with the help of U.S. antiaircraft missiles.

The Withdrawal

In 1988, the United States, Pakistan, Afghanistan, and the Soviet Union signed the Geneva Accords that led to the withdrawal of Soviet troops from Afghanistan. The last remaining Soviet troops left the country the following year.

THE AFTERMATH

Although the mujahedin succeeded in driving out the Soviet troops, their country was left physically, economically, and politically destroyed. In addition, the decade-long conflict had taken a heavy toll in human life. More than a million Afghans died during the war, and between five and six million people fled to neighboring countries as refugees or were displaced internally. About ten thousand Soviet soldiers were killed and thousands more injured. Afghanistan soon fell into a state of anarchy in which mujahedin factions that had cooperated against the Soviets split along ethnic lines and began fighting among themselves, ultimately leading Afghanistan into civil war.

Traditional Clothes

Men's Clothing

The ordinary outfit of Afghan men is a loose, long-sleeved shirt that reaches the knees and a pair of baggy trousers with a drawstring at the waist. These shirts and wide-legged trousers are usually white, black, gray, or brown. When it is cool, men often wear thick woolen vests over their shirts. During the winter months, depending on a man's ethnic group or where he comes from, he will wear either a bright woolen shawl; a *postin* (poss-TEEN), which is a sheepskin coat; or a *chapan* (cha-PAN), a long quilted robe. Well-made, heavy-duty shoes are a luxury for most rural Afghans; thin leather slippers crafted by local shoemakers are what most can afford.

Regional Headwear

Afghan men cover their heads with a range of headwear from turbans to round caps. The majority of men wear a turban that is wrapped around the locally favored type of skullcap. Pashtun men tie their turbans so one end of the cloth hangs down, while

A UNIFYING FIGURE

Since coming into office, interim leader Hamid Karzai (*above*) has helped promote unity within Afghanistan by wearing a selection of clothes that reflects the country's diverse ethnic groups. For example, his colorful robe, or chapan, is typically worn by Uzbeks and Turkmens, while his lambskin hat is popular with men living in the city of Kabul.

Left: The way in which an Afghan man wears his turban can indicate to which ethnic group he belongs. The man on the right is a Pashtun, as his turban is fastened so that one end of the cloth hangs down.

men from most other parts of the country tuck in the end. Turbans were traditionally white but now can be any color. While working in the fields, men remove their turbans and wear only their skullcaps. The *pakol* (pah-COAL) hat has become increasingly popular in recent years. Originally worn by Nuristani men, the pakol hat was adopted by the mujahedin guerrillas as a sign of resistance against the government.

Above: **These women in the central province of Bamian are dressed in the traditional clothes worn by Afghan women.**

Women's Clothing

Afghan women wear a dress or a long, loose shirt with a skirt over a baggy pair of trousers. In winter, Afghan women wrap themselves in warm wool shawls to keep out the cold. Unlike the men, most Afghan women wear clothes with varying bright colors and designs. In keeping with Islamic ideals of modesty, many Afghan women wear cotton or silk headscarves. At times, the chadari has been part of women's formal wear.

Many women also adorn themselves in heavy jewelry. Large, medallion-like necklaces and hair ornaments are made from gold, silver, and lapis lazuli. Turquoise rocks are widely used in Afghan jewelry because they are believed to ward off evil spirits.

CHILDRENSWEAR

Children dress much like their parents, although they sometimes have intricate and brightly colored embroidery on their shirts. Afghan children are known for their bright colorful hats, shawls, and vests. Toddlers typically wear long shirts and small, flat woolen caps.

Women in Afghanistan

In the twentieth century, the rights of women in Afghanistan went from one extreme to the other. Although women traditionally followed the practice of purdah, they began to enjoy greater freedoms by the 1960s and 1970s. All of these freedoms, however, were taken away during the years of Taliban rule. With the fall of the Taliban regime in late 2001, Afghan women hope their rights will be fully and permanently restored.

One Step Forward

Although Amanullah and his wife supported women's rights, the emancipation of Afghan women began in 1959 when Zahir Shah announced the voluntary end of the seclusion and veiling of women. Consequently, women in urban areas began to remove their veils, attend universities, and take part in public life.

Progress in the women's rights movement continued after the Soviet occupation, during which time women were guaranteed equal job opportunities. By the early 1990s, 70 percent of the nation's teachers, up to half of its civil servants, and 40 percent of its doctors were women. In addition, about half of the students at Kabul University were female.

Left: **These Afghan women are attending an embroidery class in December 2001. The class was organized by an Afghan non-governmental organization in the city of Kabul following the creation of the AIA.**

Left: **With the collapse of the Taliban regime, Afghan women are once again free to work outside the home. These women eat lunch at one of the few factories in Kabul that has not been destroyed by war.**

Two Steps Back

When the Taliban came to power in 1996, Afghan women and girls became virtually invisible. Girls were prohibited from receiving an education, and women were forbidden from working outside the home, except in limited circumstances in the medical field. Women were also not allowed to appear in public unless they wore a chadari and were accompanied by a male relative.

Renewed Hope

Following the defeat of the Taliban, the AIA was quick to recognize the valuable role Afghan women play in society, and two women, Dr. Sima Samar and Dr. Suhaila Siddiq, were given cabinet positions in the country's new administration. The AIA lifted the ban on girls attending schools, and women are once again allowed to work outside the home. In addition, women are no longer forced to wear a chadari although many women still choose to do so for safety reasons.

Together with women's organizations and aid agencies, the government is now focusing on ways to revitalize education, provide livelihood skills, and improve healthcare facilities for girls and women. Although it is gradual, change is coming for the women of Afghanistan. It is hoped that a democratic government will be established that will represent and promote the leadership of women in the planning and governing of the country.

THE STORY OF AN AFGHAN GIRL

In 1985, the face of an unknown Afghan girl appeared on the cover of *National Geographic* magazine. With her piercing green eyes, the young girl quickly became a worldwide symbol of the plight of Afghan women as well as refugees forced to flee their war-torn homeland. Seventeen years after the photograph was taken in a refugee camp in Pakistan, *National Geographic* managed to track the girl down. Named Sharbat Gula, she now lives her life in purdah in a remote part of Afghanistan with her husband and three daughters.

71

Ahmad Zahir

Ahmad Zahir is regarded by Afghans as a musical legend. His deep voice, charismatic good looks, and soothing melodies captured the hearts of the nation. During the late 1960s, Zahir's music was uplifting, expressing the peaceful and prosperous time in Afghan history. By the late 1970s, Zahir's therapeutic and patriotic songs endeared him even more to a population living in increasingly uncertain times.

From Nightingale of Habibia to National Star

Zahir was born on June 13, 1946, into a prominent Afghan family. Despite family pressures, Zahir chose to pursue his passion for music and strove to become a professional musician. At a very

Left: **Still an extremely popular singer today, the late Ahmad Zahir mesmerized audiences with his unique style of music. He kept up to date with music trends and enjoyed listening to music from all over the world.**

Left: **Since the fall of the Taliban regime in late 2001, music shops have reopened throughout Afghanistan. These shops sell albums of popular Afghan musicians, including Ahmad Zahir.**

young age, Zahir understood the importance of body language during a performance. Consequently, he memorized his lyrics and used graceful head and hand gestures to captivate his audience. Zahir's passion for music and professional attitude made him the most popular act at Habibia High School concerts in Kabul, and he soon became known as the Nightingale of Habibia.

After his father was appointed Afghanistan's ambassador to India, Zahir moved to Delhi with the rest of his family. There, he studied under many great Indian musical masters.

Returning to Afghanistan in 1969, Zahir worked hard to incorporate both Dari and Pashto lyrics and rhythms into his music. In addition, his lyrics touched on issues to which Afghans could relate. By 1973, Zahir's popularity had soared.

During his career, Zahir wrote and sang numerous songs that denounced the country's government and individual political figures. Although these controversial songs made him more popular with the Afghan people, they were banned by the government. Zahir was killed in a car accident in 1979.

The Legend Lives On!

Since his tragic death, Zahir has embodied the Afghans' feelings of loss. More than twenty years after his death, Zahir's music still remains in the hearts of Afghans young and old, and he continues to be recognized as one of the greatest of Afghan entertainers.

RELATIONS WITH NORTH AMERICA

The strategic location of Afghanistan in Central Asia has made the country's stability important to North America, most notably to the United States during the Cold War period. Relations between Afghanistan, the United States, and Canada were warm until the 1970s. At the outbreak of the Soviet-Afghan War, however, Canada severed diplomatic ties with Afghanistan, while the U.S. government supported mujahedin guerrillas who opposed the Soviet-backed Afghan government. After the emergence of the Taliban regime in the mid-1990s, North American relations with Afghanistan had reached an all-time low.

Opposite: **Before war broke out in Afghanistan in 1979, some shop signs in the city of Kabul also appeared in English for the benefit of North American tourists who visited the country.**

Following the fall of the Taliban regime and the establishment of the interim administration, the relationship between the three nations has entered a new stage. With the interim administration and the rest of the international community, the United States and Canada are working to establish a stable and democratic Afghanistan. Canadian and U.S. involvement in the ongoing military action in Afghanistan also has heightened the awareness of the American and Canadian peoples to the plight of the Afghans. As a result, many North Americans now are involved in humanitarian projects aimed at helping the Afghan population.

Above: **Afghans and North Americans work together on programs to remove the land mines that are scattered throughout the Afghan countryside.**

Historical Ties

In the 1830s, Josiah Harlan, an adventurer from Pennsylvania, was the first American who made extensive contact with Afghanistan. Diplomatic relations between Afghanistan and the United States, however, were officially established in 1934, a year after Zahir Shah became the king of Afghanistan.

Afghanistan remained neutral during World War II. The country's strategic position during the Cold War period, however, made it a large recipient of aid from both the United States and the Soviet Union. Between 1950 and 1979, the United States provided Afghanistan with over U.S. $500 million to help the nation develop its infrastructure and economy.

Following the 1973 coup that deposed the Afghan monarchy, tensions between the United States and the Soviet Union increased over the political stability of Afghanistan. With U.S. backing, neighboring Pakistan increased aid to Islamic movements that opposed Daud Khan's regime, while the Soviet Union funded anti-Daud Khan communist factions. Relations between Afghanistan and Canada and the United States deteriorated after the 1978 coup that brought the Soviet-backed communist government of Noor Mohammad Taraki to power. In 1979, the U.S. ambassador to Afghanistan, Adolph Dubs, was killed in Kabul. In response, the United States reduced aid to the country and downgraded its diplomatic presence in Kabul. Canada severed diplomatic ties with Afghanistan following the Soviet invasion and did not renew relations with any of the various regimes that held power after the Soviet withdrawal from Afghanistan in 1989.

Fearing the spread of Soviet influence over the rest of Central Asia, the United States, along with Saudi Arabia and Pakistan, started to provide extensive financial and military aid to mujahedin guerrillas who were fighting the occupying Soviet troops. In 1988, the United States, the Soviet Union, Pakistan, and Afghanistan signed an agreement, known as the 1988 Geneva Accords, that effectively ended the Soviet-Afghan War. Apart from guaranteeing the withdrawal of all Soviet troops by 1989, the agreement also called for U.S. and Soviet noninterference in the internal affairs of Afghanistan and Pakistan. Even before the last Soviet troops withdrew from Afghanistan in February 1989, the United States closed its embassy in Kabul for security reasons.

Above: In September 1963, Afghanistan's Zahir Shah (*left*) traveled to the United States, where he met President John F. Kennedy (*right*).

Opposite: This Afghan mujahedin fighter protects his position in the Hindu Kush Range against Soviet troops during the Soviet-Afghan War. The United States and other nations provided weapons to the mujahedin.

Strained Relations during the 1990s

Both the United States and Canada condemned the Taliban regime that had come to control most of Afghanistan by 1996, after emerging as the strongest faction during the Afghan civil war. The U.S. and Canadian governments refused to recognize the Taliban as Afghanistan's legitimate government, and both nations were critical of the Taliban's human rights violations, particularly directed against women and girls.

Relations between the United States and Afghanistan soured even further following the bombing of U.S. embassies in Kenya and Tanzania in August 1998. The bombings were allegedly masterminded by Saudi Arabian militant Osama bin Laden, who was living in Afghanistan as a guest of the Taliban. In retaliation, the United States launched missiles at training bases in Afghanistan that were reportedly connected to Al-Qaeda, an international terrorist organization believed to be run by bin Laden. In addition, the United States continued to oppose both the Taliban's request for international recognition as the official government of Afghanistan and their attempts to gain control of Afghanistan's seat in the U.N. General Assembly in New York. The United States and Canada also joined the international community in condemning the Taliban's destruction of the world-famous Buddha statues at Bamian in March 2001.

SANCTIONS

Following the Taliban's refusal to extradite Osama bin Laden, the United States imposed sanctions against the Taliban in July 1999. These sanctions froze the Taliban's assets in the United States and banned all exchange of goods, apart from humanitarian aid, in an attempt to force the Taliban to hand over bin Laden for trial. The U.N. also imposed sanctions on the Taliban in November 1999. These sanctions froze Taliban assets and prohibited international flights to or from Taliban territory, effectively grounding Ariana Afghan Airlines, Afghanistan's national airline. After strong pressure from the United States and Russia, the U.N. strengthened sanctions by imposing an arms embargo as well in 2000.

Left: Ousted Afghan president Burhanuddin Rabbani (*standing*), who led the country from 1992 to 1996, continued to hold the Afghan seat in the U.N. General Assembly even after the Taliban's rise to power in Afghanistan. Factions loyal to Rabbani controlled about 10 percent of Afghanistan, mainly in the northern parts of the country, during the rule of the Taliban.

Left: **U.S. marines from the Light Armored Reconnaissance (LAR) Battalion drive Light Armored Vehicles (LAVs) near the American military compound at the airport in Kandahar in January 2002.**

War on Terrorism

Following the terrorist attacks on the United States on September 11, 2001, the United States identified Osama bin Laden as the prime suspect. In the weeks following the attacks, the Taliban refused repeatedly to extradite bin Laden and members of the Al-Qaeda network. As a result, U.S. president George W. Bush announced air strikes against Afghanistan, and a U.S.-led coalition against terrorism began its military campaign on October 7, 2001. Aerial bombardments targeted terrorist facilities and various Taliban military and political centers within Afghanistan.

As the U.N. was forced to suspend most of its aid programs in Afghanistan due to the air strikes, U.S. forces also conducted air drops of food and medical supplies as part of a humanitarian relief effort to help the Afghan people. With the support of the U.S.-led coalition, Northern Alliance forces advanced through the country, and, in late November 2001, the first U.S. ground forces landed near the city of Kandahar in southern Afghanistan. The Taliban surrendered their last stronghold in December 2001, and the U.S.-led offensive then focused its efforts on defeating Al-Qaeda fighters who were taking refuge in the mountains in eastern Afghanistan.

Both Canadian and U.S. troops worked together on various military operations against Taliban and Al-Qaeda forces. These operations included Operation Anaconda, which took place in March 2002.

Below: **Following the beginning of military strikes by U.S. and British forces within Afghanistan, U.S. forces flying over Afghanistan dropped leaflets, such as the one below, to assure the Afghan population that the bombing was aimed at ridding the nation of terrorists. Written in both Dari and Pashto, the text on the front of the leaflet reads, "The Partnership of Nations is here to help," while the text on the back of the leaflet reads, "The Partnership of Nations is here to assist the People of Afghanistan."**

Left: Afghanistan's Hamid Karzai (*left*) and U.S. president George W. Bush (*right*) hold a press conference at the White House in Washington, D.C., on January 28, 2002.

SANCTIONS

On January 15, 2002, the U.N. Security Council lifted the air embargo against Afghanistan, which meant Ariana Afghan Airlines could once again fly to overseas destinations. The following day, the U.N. issued a resolution that kept the remaining sanctions against Afghanistan in place for a period of 12 months.

Current Relations: A New Era

Both the United States and Canada have reestablished diplomatic ties with Afghanistan following the creation of the interim administration. Since then, there has been an exchange of official visitors between Afghanistan and the North American nations. On January 17, 2002, U.S. secretary of state Colin Powell became the first U.S. secretary of state to visit Afghanistan in twenty-five years, while Canadian deputy prime minister John Manley visited Afghanistan on January 25, 2002. Afghan interim leader Hamid Karzai traveled to the United States in January 2002 to hold meetings with U.S. president George W. Bush.

The U.S. and Canadian governments have pledged their continued support of humanitarian, transition, and reconstruction programs within Afghanistan. Furthermore, in May 2002, U.S. president George W. Bush restored normal trade relations with Afghanistan, which had been suspended since 1986. Officials hope the restoration of trade ties will contribute to economic growth and assist Afghanistan in rebuilding its economy. American and Canadian troops also are present in Afghanistan. These soldiers are helping maintain law and order as well as continuing the military offensive aimed at capturing any remaining members of the Al-Qaeda terrorist network.

BUSINESS AS USUAL

Both the Afghan embassy in Washington and the U.S. embassy in Kabul were reopened at the beginning of 2002. U.S. secretary of state Colin Powell officiated at the reopening of the U.S. embassy in Kabul, which had been closed since 1989 for security reasons. The Afghan embassy in Washington was officially reopened on January 28, 2002, after being closed by the U.S. State Department in August 1997. The reopening ceremony was attended by Afghan interim leader Hamid Karzai and U.S. deputy secretary of state Richard Armitage, among others.

Immigration to North America

The first large wave of Afghan emigration to North America began shortly after Soviet troops invaded Afghanistan in 1979. Most of the Afghans who fled their homeland were academics and professionals who were trained to be doctors, educators, scientists, and engineers. These Afghans originally believed they would be able to return to Afghanistan within a few months or years as they thought the Soviet occupation would not last long.

The second wave of immigrants from Afghanistan began to arrive in North America when the communist-supported Afghan government collapsed in 1992 and internal fighting broke out between rival mujahedin factions. By that time, many Afghan cities had become too dangerous to live in, and most schools had either been destroyed or closed down due to repeated bombings. The third wave of Afghan emigration occurred after the emergence of the Taliban regime in the mid-1990s. These Afghan immigrants fled their homeland because they feared persecution by the Taliban due to ethnic ties, religion, or political beliefs. All of these waves of Afghan immigrants tended to settle in North American metropolitan areas, such as Ontario, New York, and Washington, D.C. The main reasons they settled in to these areas included the availability of jobs and the existence of small Afghan communities.

RETURNING HOME

During his visit to the United States in January 2002, Afghan interim leader Hamid Karzai called on Afghan expatriates living in North America to return to Afghanistan and help rebuild the war-torn nation. Since then, Afghan-North Americans, including writers, fashion designers, and engineers, have answered his call to return to their native land. Most of these volunteers have signed up with nonprofit organizations, such as the International Organization for Migration — Return of Qualified Afghans Programme (IOM-RQA), to participate in short- or long-term volunteer programs in Afghanistan.

Left: Members of RAWA hold a press conference in New York in December 2001 to highlight their campaign aimed at achieving equal rights for the women of Afghanistan.

81

North Americans in Afghanistan

Prior to the outbreak of war in 1979, Afghanistan's breathtaking landscape, historical sites, and hospitable people drew hundreds of North American tourists to the country. Since the 1980s, most of the North Americans who have traveled to Afghanistan have been volunteers working with aid organizations such as the International Committee of the Red Cross, the Canadian International Development Agency (CIDA), and the U.S. Agency for International Development (USAID).

Humanitarian Aid

International aid has played an important role in helping to alleviate the suffering of Afghans affected by over two decades of war, poverty, famine, and three years of drought. The United States is the world's leading humanitarian aid donor to Afghanistan and has pledged nearly U.S. $300 million in humanitarian assistance for 2002. Between 1990 and 2001, Canada provided Afghanistan with U.S. $160 million in humanitarian aid and pledged a further U.S. $100 million in January 2002.

CIDA programs in Afghanistan focus on providing basic health care and education; promoting human rights, notably

A HUMANITARIAN CRISIS

During the Soviet-Afghan War, millions of Afghan refugees fled across the border to Pakistan and Iran, and more than half of the population was displaced internally. By the end of the war, Afghanistan's economy was crippled; the school system was largely destroyed, irrigation projects were badly damaged, and industrialization was seriously limited. The plight of the Afghan people was further exacerbated by the subsequent civil war. The number of civilians fleeing the country increased, creating the world's worst refugee crisis. Already suffering the devastating effects of civil war, the Afghan people also faced a series of natural disasters that began in the late 1990s, including earthquakes, flooding, and drought. Following the U.S.-led fight against terrorism, even more Afghans fled their homes to escape military strikes by U.S. and British forces, thus making the Afghan humanitarian crisis even more desperate.

Left: Afghan women sit patiently in front of the U.N. World Food Programme (WFP) headquarters in Kabul in the hope of receiving food aid.

the rights of women; assisting with land mine removal; reintegrating people returning to their homes; and supporting peace efforts. USAID sponsors numerous programs aimed to improve the Afghan people's quality of life, including public health education on hygiene, malnutrition, and maternal and child care as well as training for Afghan farmers in agricultural techniques and animal husbandry. In addition, USAID is involved in programs to rebuild roads and bridges, construct and repair irrigation and water supply systems, and provide water pumping systems that will give the Afghan people drinkable water.

Both the United States and Canada are members of the Afghanistan Support Group (ASG). Founded by the European Union (EU) and the fifteen largest donor countries to Afghanistan, the ASG works to provide international support for Afghanistan. The ASG supports programs related to economic and social development, education, and the reconstruction of the country.

America's Fund for Afghan Children

In October 2001, U.S. president George W. Bush appealed to American children to donate U.S. $1 to help support the more than ten million children in Afghanistan whose lives have been devastated by years of conflict and civil unrest. Organized by the American Red Cross, the money donated is used to provide food, shelter, and medicine urgently needed by Afghan children.

BASIC AID

Although international aid organizations are involved in long-term initiatives aimed to help improve the living conditions of the Afghan people, these organizations also provide urgently needed items such as water, blankets, cooking utensils, clothes, shelter, and food.

Left: This Afghan-American has displayed an American flag outside his store in the Little Kabul area of Fremont, California, to show his support for the U.S.-led coalition against terrorism.

Afghans in North America

About 200,000 Afghans make their home in the United States, and vibrant Afghan communities exist in New York, Washington, Los Angeles, and the San Francisco Bay area. An estimated fifty to sixty thousand Afghans have settled in Canada, the majority of whom live in Ontario.

North America's Afghan community plays an active role in promoting and nurturing its culture through organizations and committees. Founded in 1996 by retired congressman Don Ritter, the Afghanistan-America Foundation (AAF) is a nonprofit organization that was established to create American-Afghan ties through educational, economic, and social programs. The organization now has an office in Kabul, and its members are actively participating in reconstruction projects in Afghanistan. The Afghan Youth Organization (AYO), which is based in Canada, aims to increase the awareness of young Afghans who have grown up in Canada about their cultural heritage.

Organizations have been set up to help Afghans who have settled in either the United States or Canada adapt to their new surroundings as well as to provide support to Afghan professionals seeking employment. A number of Afghan-North American associations also participate in medical relief and other charitable activities that help people in Afghanistan and Afghan refugees living in camps in Pakistan and Iran.

LITTLE KABUL

Fremont, California, is home to the largest Afghan community in the United States, and one section of the town's Fremont Boulevard is known as Little Kabul. Along this stretch of the boulevard are Afghan restaurants, a kabob stand, grocery stores that sell halal meats and the sweet green melons native to Afghanistan, and many businesses run by Afghan-Americans.

Afghans Influence North Americans

Although Afghan-North Americans have generally assimilated into North American society, they still retain their cultural identity by fostering aspects of their heritage. Nearly every city with a sizable Afghan community has restaurants, bakeries, and shops selling Afghan foods, spices, and goods.

North Americans have a growing interest in a variety of Afghan products and handicrafts, including hand-woven carpets. Many of these carpets are made by Afghan women and girls living in refugee camps in Pakistan. Widely bought carpets include the Afghan war rugs that first emerged during the Soviet-Afghan War. These rugs feature images of war that include helicopters, jet airplanes, and tanks.

Academic Ties

Educational institutions exist throughout North America that offer language courses in Dari and Pashto as well as courses in Islamic studies. The University of Nebraska at Omaha is home to the Center for Afghanistan Studies, the only center of its kind in the country. In addition, the university's library houses the Arthur Paul Afghanistan Collection, a large collection of materials about Afghan life and culture.

FARHAD DARYA

Born on September 22, 1962, Farhad Darya is one of Afghanistan's most prominent contemporary singers, songwriters, and composers. Through his music, Darya spoke out against the Soviet occupation of his nation, and his songs quickly became popular with the Afghan population, including the mujahedin fighters. As a result, many of his songs were banned by the communist-backed Afghan government. Darya left Afghanistan in 1990 and moved to the United States in 1995. He tours extensively throughout the United States and Canada.

Left: Both Afghan and American goods are on sale at this shop located on the stretch of Fremont Boulevard known as Little Kabul.

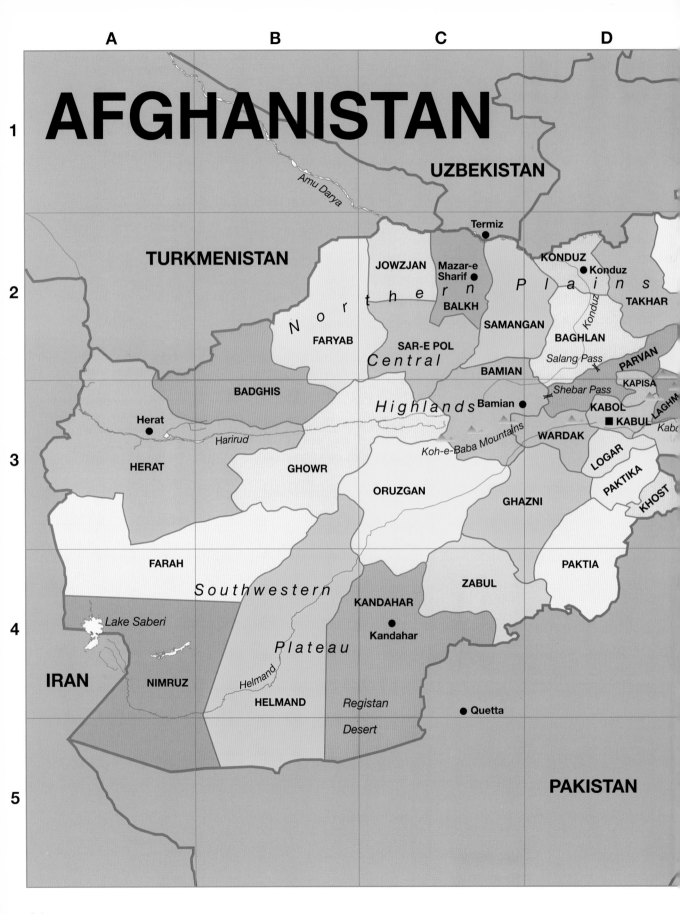

AFGHANISTAN

A   B   C   D

1

UZBEKISTAN

TURKMENISTAN

Termiz

KONDUZ

2

JOWZJAN   Mazar-e Sharif   Konduz

BALKH   TAKHAR

N o r t h e r n   P l a i n s

FARYAB   SAMANGAN   Konduz

SAR-E POL   BAGHLAN

C e n t r a l   Salang Pass   PARVAN

BAMIAN   KAPISA

Shebar Pass

BADGHIS   H i g h l a n d s   Bamian   KABOL

Herat   KABUL   LAGHM

Harirud   Koh-e-Baba Mountains   WARDAK   Kabu

3

HERAT   GHOWR   LOGAR

ORUZGAN   PAKTIKA

GHAZNI   KHOST

PAKTIA

FARAH   S o u t h w e s t e r n   ZABUL

KANDAHAR

4

Lake Saberi   P l a t e a u   Kandahar

IRAN   NIMRUZ   Helmand

HELMAND   Registan

Desert   Quetta

5

PAKISTAN

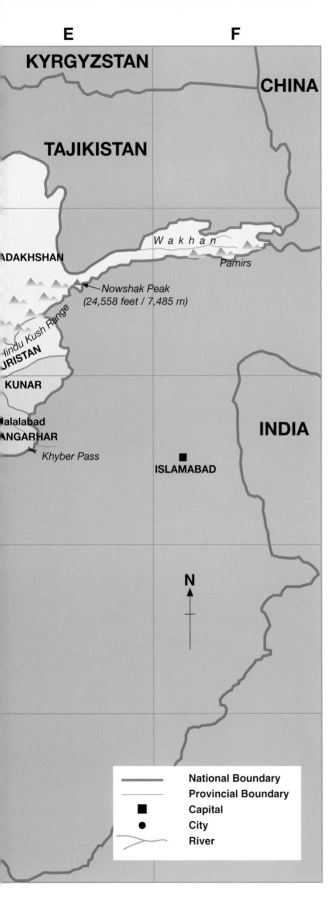

E   **F**

KYRGYZSTAN

CHINA

TAJIKISTAN

Wakhan

Pamirs

ADAKHSHAN

→ *Nowshak Peak*
(24,558 feet / 7,485 m)

Hindu Kush Range

URISTAN

KUNAR

alalabad

ANGARHAR

Khyber Pass

INDIA

■ ISLAMABAD

N
↑

───	National Boundary
───	Provincial Boundary
■	Capital
●	City
∿	River

Amu Darya River A1–F2

Badakhshan (province)
   D1–E2
Badghis (province)
   A2–B3
Baghlan (province)
   D2–D3
Balkh (province) C2
Bamian (city) C3
Bamian (province) C2–D3

Central Highlands
   (region) C2–C3
China F1–F2

Farah (province) A3–B4
Faryab (province) B2–C2

Ghazni (province) C3–D4
Ghowr (province) B3–C2

Harirud River A2–C3
Helmand (province)
   B3–B5
Helmand River A4–D3
Herat (city) A3
Herat (province) A2–B3
Hindu Kush Range
   D3–E2

India D5–F2
Iran A2–A5
Islamabad F3

Jalalabad E3
Jowzjan (province) C2

Kabol (province) D3
Kabul D3
Kabul River D3–E3
Kandahar (city) C4
Kandahar (province)
   B4–C5
Kapisa (province) D2–D3
Khost (province) D3
Khyber Pass E3
Koh-e-Baba Mountains
   C3
Konduz (province) D2
Konduz (city) D2
Konduz River C3–D2

Kunar (province) E2–E3
Kyrgyzstan D1–F1

Laghman (province)
   D2–E3
Lake Saberi A4
Logar (province) D3

Mazar-e Sharif C2

Nangarhar (province)
   D3–E3
Nimruz (province) A4–B5
Northern Plains (region)
   B2–D2
Nowshak Peak E2
Nuristan (province)
   D2–E2

Oruzgan (province)
   B3–C4

Pakistan A5–F2
Paktia (province) D3–D4
Paktika (province) D3
Pamirs F2
Parvan (province) D2–D3

Quetta C4

Registan Desert B4–C5

Salang Pass D2
Samangan (province)
   C2–D2
Sar-e Pol (province)
   C2–C3
Shebar Pass D3
Southwestern Plateau
   (region) B4–C4

Tajikistan C1–F2
Takhar (province) D2
Termiz C2
Turkmenistan A1–C2

Uzbekistan A1–C2

Wakhan (region) F2
Wardak (province) C3–D3

Zabul (province) C3–D4

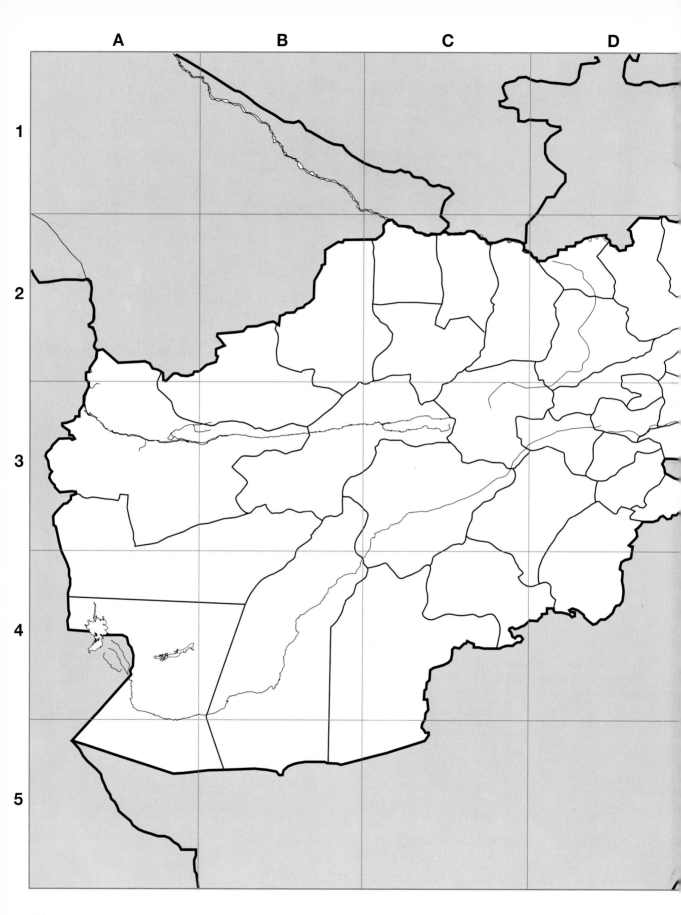

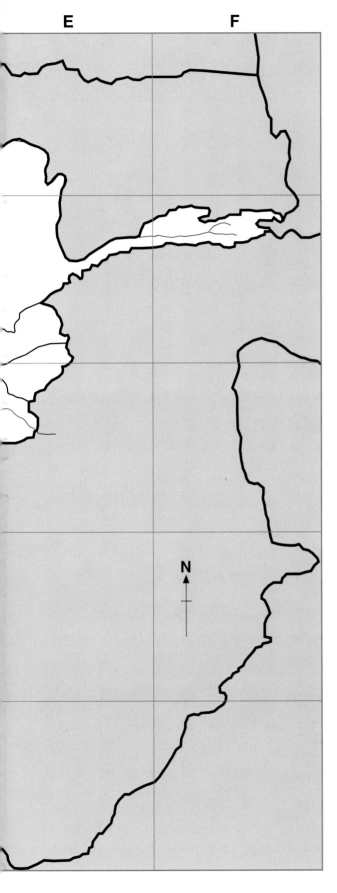

E F

N

How Is Your Geography?

Learning to identify the main geographical areas and points of a country can be challenging. Although it may seem difficult at first to memorize the locations and spellings of major cities or the names of mountain ranges, rivers, deserts, lakes, and other prominent physical features, the end result of this effort can be very rewarding. Places you previously did not know existed will suddenly come to life when referred to in world news, whether in newspapers, television reports, other books and reference sources, or on the Internet. This knowledge will make you feel a bit closer to the rest of the world, with its fascinating variety of cultures and physical geography.

Used in a classroom setting, the instructor can make duplicates of this map using a copy machine. (PLEASE DO NOT WRITE IN THIS BOOK!) Students can then fill in any requested information on their individual map copies. Used one-on-one, the student can also make copies of the map on a copy machine and use them as a study tool. The student can practice identifying place names and geographical features on his or her own.

Afghanistan at a Glance

Official Name   Islamic State of Afghanistan

Capital   Kabul

Official Languages   Dari, Pashto

Population   26,813,057 (July 2001 estimate)

Land Area   250,000 square miles (647,500 sq km)

Provinces   Badakhshan, Badghis, Baghlan, Balkh, Bamian, Farah, Faryab, Ghazni, Ghowr, Helmand, Herat, Jowzjan, Kabol, Kandahar, Kapisa, Khost, Konduz, Kunar, Laghman, Logar, Nangarhar, Nimruz, Nuristan, Oruzgan, Paktia, Paktika, Parvan, Samangan, Sar-e Pol, Takhar, Wardak, Zabul

Highest Point   Nowshak Peak 24,558 feet (7,485 m)

Border Countries   China, Iran, Pakistan, Tajikistan, Turkmenistan, Uzbekistan

Major Rivers   Amu Darya, Harirud, Helmand, Kabul

Major Lake   Saberi

Major Cities   Herat, Kabul, Kandahar, Mazar-e Sharif

Official Religion   Islam

Festivals   Nawruz (March 21)

Labor Day (May 1)

Remembrance Day for the Martyrs and the Disabled (May 4)

Independence Day (August 19)

Main Exports   Cotton, fruits and nuts, handwoven carpets, hides and pelts, precious and semi-precious gems, wool

Main Imports   Consumer goods, food, and petroleum products

Currency   Afghani (42,000 AFA = U.S. $1 in May 2002)

Opposite: Lush green valleys in Afghanistan's Central Highlands give way to snow-capped mountains.

Glossary

(Note: Words followed by an asterisk are common to both Dari and Pashto.)

Arabic Vocabulary

mehrab (MEH-rahb): an arch in a mosque that indicates the direction of Mecca, Islam's most sacred city.

menber (MUHN-brr): a many-tiered pulpit.

Dari Vocabulary

aush (AHSH): a soup made with noodles, yogurt, kidney beans, and chickpeas and flavored with dill, turmeric, and mint.

aushak (AHSH-ak): leek- and onion-filled ravioli topped with yogurt, mint, and a meat sauce.

baba-kalan (BAH-bah-KAH-lawn): "older father"; a name for a grandparent.

bebejan (BEE-BEE-jawn): "my sweet dear"; a name for a grandparent.

bujul-bazi (buh-JULL-bah-ZEE): a game that resembles marbles but is played with sheep's knuckles.

buzkashi (BOOZ-kah-SHEE): "goat pulling"; a game in which opposing teams try to gain control of and drop the body of a goat or calf into the designated scoring area.

chadaris (CHA-dah-REES): garments worn by Muslim women that cover them from head to toe; also known as burqas.

chapan (cha-PAN): a long quilted robe.

chapandaz (cha-PAN-dawz): a skilled horseman that plays buzkashi.

dogh (DOUGH): a yogurt drink.

*dowl** (DOWL): a type of drum.

dutar (DEW-tar): a fourteen-stringed lute.

Eid al-Adha (EED AHL-ad-ah): the Feast of the Sacrifice.

Eid al-Fitr (EED AHL-fitr): the Muslim festival celebrated at the end of Ramazan, the Muslim month of fasting.

gudiparan bazi (GOO-dee-PAH-RON bah-ZEE): kite flying.

haft-mehwah (HAFT-MAY-wah): a mixture of seven fruits and nuts that symbolizes spring.

*jin** (JIN): a creature that appears in Afghan folklore.

karez (CAH-rahz): an irrigation system of tunnels, trenches, and wells that channels water to low-lying areas.

Nawruz (NOW-rooz): the Afghan New Year, which falls on the first day of spring.

pahlwani (pahl-wah-KNEE): wrestling.

*pakol** (pah-COAL): a type of hat that was originally worn by Nuristani men. Mujahedin guerrillas adopted this hat as a sign of resistance during the Soviet-Afghan War.

postin (poss-TEEN): a sheepskin coat.

qarajai (CAH-rah-JYE): a variation of buzkashi in which the horseman drags the body of a goat or calf around a marker and then returns the carcass to the team's designated scoring circle.

quabili pallow (KAH-bih-lee pah-LOW): a baked rice dish made with chicken or lamb, onions, carrots, raisins, pistachios, and almonds.

Ramazan (RAM-ah-ZAHN): the Muslim month of fasting; also called Ramadan.

rubab (ruh-BAHB): a banjo-like instrument played by plucking the strings.

sabzi challow (saab-ZEE cha-LOW): a rice dish consisting of spinach and lamb.

samanak (SAH-MAN-ak): a dessert made of wheat and sugar.

tanbur (TAN-bur): a long-necked lute.

tar (TAHR): string that is attached to an Afghan kite.

topay-danda (TOE-pay-DAN-dah): a game similar to stickball.

tudabarai (TOO-dee-bah-REE): a variation of buzkashi in which the horseman gains possession of the body of a goat or calf and then carries it away from the starting circle in any direction to gain points.

Pashto Vocabulary

attan (AH-tan): the national dance of Afghanistan.

loya jirga (LOY-ah jir-GAH): "grand assembly"; a unique Afghan institution in which ethnic elders come together to discuss issues of national importance.

pashtunwali (PASH-tuhn-wah-lee): the Pashtun code of honor, courage, and self-pride that is followed by all Afghans.

talib (TAH-lib): "student"; the word from which *Taliban* is derived.

English Vocabulary

abdicated: gave up or renounced a throne, right, or power, in a formal manner.

anarchy: political and social disorder due to the absence of governmental control.

autonomy: self-government.

bicameral: consisting of two legislative chambers or houses.

buffer: a nation or area of land that lies between larger and potentially hostile nations.

coup d'état: unexpected political uprising.

eclectic: wide-ranging; coming from many different sources.

equestrian: related to horseback riding.

flanked: placed or posted at the side of.

guerrillas: soldiers who form an unofficial army to fight against an existing political order.

infrastructure: the system of public works and utilities of a country.

interim: temporary; provisional.

leftist: advocating reform in politics, usually against the traditional order.

martyrdom: the act of suffering or dying for a religious cause.

mujahedin: "holy warriors"; Muslim guerrillas, especially in Afghanistan.

plundered: robbed goods or valuables forcefully from a place, as in war.

purdah: the practice of secluding women from public observation.

Richter scale: a logarithmic scale used to express the magnitude of an earthquake.

stalemate: a situation where no action can be taken or progress made; deadlock.

stupas: dome-shaped mounds or monuments used as Buddhist shrines.

subsistence farming: farming that provides for the farm family's needs with little surplus for selling.

suffrage: the right to vote.

tectonic: related to the structure of the Earth's surface or crust.

More Books to Read

Afghanistan. Cultures of the World series. Sharifah Enayat Ali (Benchmark Books)

Afghanistan: Modern Nations of the World series. Laurel Corona (Lucent Books)

Afghanistan in Pictures. Visual Geography series. Camille Mirepoix (Lerner)

The Breadwinner. Deborah Ellis (Groundwood-Douglas & McIntyre)

Islam. World Beliefs and Cultures series. Sue Penney (Heinemann)

Muslim Festival Tales. Festival Tales series. Kerena Marchant (Raintree/Steck-Vaughn)

My Forbidden Face: Growing Up Under the Taliban: A Young Woman's Story. Latifa
    (Talk Miramax)

Operation Enduring Freedom. War on Terrorism series. John Hamilton
    (Abdo & Daughters)

The Silk Route: 7,000 Miles of History. John S. Major (HarperTrophy)

Videos

Afghanistan Revealed. (National Geographic)

Afghanistan: The Vicious Circle. (NimaFilm)

Beneath the Borqa in Afghanistan. (Caipirinha Productions)

In the Footsteps of Alexander the Great. (PBS)

Web Sites

kidsfund.redcross.org/learn.html

www.afghan-info.com/Afghistory.htm

www.afghanland.com/home/home.html

www.afghanpeople.com/

www.afghan-web.com/

Due to the dynamic nature of the Internet, some web sites stay current longer than others. To find additional web sites, use a reliable search engine with one or more of the following keywords to help you locate information about Afghanistan. Keywords: *Dari, Hamid Karzai, Hindu Kush Range, Kabul,* loya jirga, *mujahedin, Zahir Shah, Taliban.*

Index